MISSILES and the Revolution in Warfare

MISSILES and the

NELS A. PARSON, Jr.

Revolution in Warfare

HARVARD UNIVERSITY PRESS

Cambridge, Massachusetts · 1962

This book has been reviewed by the Department of
Defense and has been officially released for open
publication. The opinions and conclusions are
those of the author and not necessarily those of
any military service.

Library of Congress Catalog Card Number 62-19221
Printed in the United States of America

Preface

Whenever missiles are discussed, the questions still urgently asked are, "Will guided missiles bring push-button warfare? Do they make other weapons obsolete? What defense is there against them?" The purpose of this book is to answer these questions about missiles by surveying their development history, describing their technical characteristics, and analyzing their revolutionary impact on military operations.

It is now generally accepted that missiles in one form or another will be used by nearly all combat forces. Missiles already have appeared in such roles as that of antitank weapon, field artillery, air- and missile-defense weapon, aircraft bomb, and torpedo. All military services will use missiles, guided and unguided, and should another major war come, everyone in or out of uniform will be affected by them.

This book is the outgrowth of an earlier volume, *Guided Missiles in War and Peace,* published originally in 1956. The aim of that book and of this one is to present to military and civil leaders, and to the general public, a basic introduction to missiles and their probable effects on military operations and on the civilian populace. Some technical portions of the earlier book remain unchanged and have been retained in this version for the convenience of the reader; by including them, I adhere to my goal of presenting the subject in a single package. However, the book as a whole represents a completely new analysis of the revolution in warfare that missiles have brought about. On occasion I go a little further and propose the development of new materiel, organization, or operational concepts to cope with that revolution.

Chapters 8 through 11 discuss in turn the employment of guided missiles in control of land areas, in control of sea areas, in strategic missile attack and defense, and in space operations. These areas were selected because the classic terms *land, naval,* and *air warfare* have become undefinable, indistinguishable, and even obsolete. The new terms cannot be separated clearly either, for that matter, but they are more useful in the light of current technology.

Warfare in these four areas is discussed objectively and without regard to the present organizational structure of the Armed Forces of the United States. The service to which a certain type of missile should belong is irrelevant to this book. For example, the reader will find the word *artillery* used in a generic sense to describe all ballistic-trajectory weapons. This term is used for technical convenience and has no relation to assignments of missiles to services. The individual military services no longer have combat missions, for that matter, only training and support roles. It is the unified and specified commands, responsible to the President through the Joint Chiefs of Staff and the Secretary of Defense, that have fighting missions.

The opinions expressed herein are mine and not necessarily those of any military service. Although many references were used in the preparation of this book, all are unclassified and public knowledge. A large part of the philosophy on future warfare is not based on references but rather on general experience and thought and was developed while I was a member of the 4th Missile Command in Korea. During this period I took part in some of the finest informal symposia (in the original Greek sense) on missiles in which I have had the pleasure of participating.

I am indebted to many persons for their assistance, criticism, and advice in the preparation of this book. I particularly wish to acknowledge the assistance of Lieutenant Colonel Donald Gruenther, U. S. Army, and Mr. Frank Williams, Marshall Space Flight Center, Huntsville, Alabama. Their helpful comments were invaluable to me.

N.A.P.

Contents

Foreword by Wernher von Braun

DIRECTOR, MARSHALL SPACE FLIGHT CENTER, HUNTSVILLE, ALABAMA

For centuries man has dreamed of traveling through space and to other celestial bodies. Now the door to this boundless new frontier has been opened and man has taken his first steps into what could be the richest blessing the Creator has yet unveiled to mankind—other than life itself.

This gift of space technology very likely will be the key to a more abundant life on this and possibly other planets; but if incorrectly used, it could lead to the total destruction of mankind. The new technology, unfortunately, must mature in a world of increasing tension between two incompatible philosophies, individual freedom and Communism.

Recent advancements in missile and space technology have been supported primarily by the military services, and all but a few of our present accomplishments in space have utilized hardware developed for insuring peace or, if necessary, for waging war. In addition to continuing the military aspects of missile and space weaponry, our nation has established a new and growing civilian space organization, the National Aeronautics and Space Administration, devoted solely to the peaceful use of space technology.

Which of this country's endeavors, peaceful or military, will be given major emphasis in the years to come and what this will mean to all of us is not known today. We can only work and pray that someday our ultimate goal, to create a climate of security within which to pursue mankind's dream of freedom under God for all men, will be realized. As this book illustrates so well, today's missile and space systems represent some of the most important struts and beams of our nation's security, and as such have an enormous impact on our lives.

The author's interest in missiles began with his participation in Project Paperclip, the U. S. program that brought my colleagues in the V-2 rocket work with me to America from Germany. In the years since, his studies and work have led to numerous contributions to missile tactics and strategy. This useful book, however, is a nontechnical introduction to be read with ease and understanding by anyone interested in missiles and space vehicles, how they can be used, and what makes them go.

1. The Revolution

Will military history ever include a description such as this?

Suddenly the smoldering conflict burst into two widely separated "local" wars, one in Africa and one in Southeast Asia. Responding to United Nations' appeals for aid to the victimized nations, the United States dispatched nearly all available forces from her homeland.

Despite heavy fighting between "volunteer" and U. S. units, and frequent use of missiles, no nuclear attacks ensued in either of the two conflicts. This was because the major powers were not directly threatened; furthermore, there was the risk of unlimited expansion of a nuclear war, a lack of good targets in the close fighting, and the certainty of alienating friendly peoples near targets. The conflict looked very much like the Korean War of the 1950's, except for the increased mobility of forces and the high toll missiles exacted on tanks, aircraft, and surface shipping.

On Friday morning of the first week in July, enemy satellite reconnaissance stepped up sharply both in quantity and in provocative low-altitude orbits over the United States. Communist armored units began to move in Western Europe. Even as the United States demanded an explanation of these actions and warned of their consequences, the first nuclear missile burst in Africa.

It was a small, tactical nuclear weapon that the enemy exploded, apparently by accident, within his own area; but it triggered a nuclear attack on U. S. forces. A series of bursts of ever-increasing size followed. Then U. S. missile-defense forces fired a nuclear missile at a falling object that had separated from a hostile satellite and appeared to be headed for Washington. An orbiting-satellite defense weapon overtook and destroyed the carrier with another blinding nuclear burst over eastern Asia.

The American moves were answered the following night with a strategic missile attack on the North American continent and an invasion of Western Europe. The missiles were first detected rising from Siberia and heading toward the northwestern United States. Off southern California, submarine-launched missiles pointed toward Los Angeles, San Diego, and Denver. Similar attacks were launched on the northeastern and north central United States.

As defensive missiles rose to meet the assault, U. S. intercontinental-ballistic-missile squadrons and missile submarines began firing in retaliation, and a frightful scene spread over the darkened North American continent. Nuclear fireballs flashed from coast to coast—many high in space, intercepted by defensive missiles, but some on the ground as well. Rocket exhausts of counterattacking missiles could be seen crawling upward into the darkness. All through the long, terrifying night the missiles came in, went out, and met in space.

When at last dawn came, it was realized that despite the fury of the night only a fraction of the incoming missiles had reached their intended targets. Radioactive fallout, though severe in many areas, was exacting a serious toll only in sections of the midwest where fallout protection had never been taken seriously. Although the damage in Eurasia was of comparable magnitude, the destruction that had come was paralyzing to both combatants. Fires, destruction, rescue operations, care of the injured, and avoidance of radioactivity dominated the scene.

Nuclear attacks of lessening intensity and recognition that survival was possible were accompanied by a grim determination to win. Allied forces in Europe, locked with the enemy in a desperate nuclear battle of missile artillery, armored forces, and infantry, held at the Rhine.

July's missile attacks were followed by the Communist invasion in August. First Alaska and points along the Canadian Pacific coast were occupied against sporadic resistance. Then submarine and seaplane troop transports assaulted a beachhead near Seattle. Rapidly expanding his perimeter to include populous areas, the enemy soon had a stronghold that U. S. forces could not attack with nuclear missiles for fear of destroying their own people.

While a newly constituted strategic reserve sought to move to the northwest and repel the invaders, the Allies began to disengage from the local conflicts a sufficient force to make a strategic assault on the enemy heartland. Thus, after a generation of feints, threats, and subversion the great world battle was under way.

Historians may well record such a nuclear war as this; it cannot be dismissed as impossible. This is the war that must be prevented, the thermonuclear holocaust that must never be allowed to come. How can we prevent it? By taking the offensive on the political, economic, and social fronts and by backing up these efforts with adequate military strength. The military backup must include a powerful strategic missile attack capability and a well-organized active and passive missile-defense system. We must also have forces to control vital air and sea lanes, means to control land areas and to protect the inhabitants from Communist insurgency, and an ability to project ground forces into the vitals of the enemy.

Nuclear-missile warfare may not spread accidentally from a limited war to a general conflict as described here. Several alternatives are possible. It may come in a massive, deliberately executed, surprise attack—although this is the least likely possibility if we have an adequate defense and are prepared to retaliate. Without both active defenses to intercept incoming missiles and passive defenses to minimize the extent of damage, the attack would be a far greater tragedy than depicted above. It might also produce unanticipated side effects. For example, deliberate nuclear attack and retaliation could abruptly reduce one or both combatants to second- or third-rate military powers and raise uninvolved nations to ascendancy.

As a second alternative, the use of nuclear missiles, especially the smaller tactical missiles, could be confined to the battle area and not cause expansion into a general nuclear war. This seems an unlikely possibility, but special circumstances or locale, such as fighting in remote uninhabited regions, at sea, or in space, might create this type of unstable situation. It is difficult to imagine it continuing, however. Either there would be tacit agreement to stop using nuclear weapons, or bigger and bigger bursts would occur until all stops were out.

Nuclear missiles may remain an unused threat, as were chemicals in World War II, but the threat of nuclear missiles will be much more imminent than was that of chemicals. Coupled with the danger of expansion into general nuclear war, it gives added deterrence to even "limited" wars; thus the rising importance of paramilitary activity. Protracted insurgency and guerrilla warfare, often involving only the most simple infantry weapons, is in part a by-product of missile technology. The very existence of the missile accentuates the bayonet.

The military paradox of our time is that, despite the race for supremacy in missilery and in space flight, savage, primitive conflict with simple weapons is the most frequent form of fighting. This is the gray war in which the world finds itself today. It is neither black nor white; yet it is very real and is not likely to end until either freedom or Communism triumphs.

Strange new possibilities in warfare have been created by modern military technology. In this second half of the twentieth century, technology has become as important to the strategist as tactics or logistics.

The implications of combat employment of missiles are profound and must be studied by all military and political leaders. The nation's leaders are already required to have a general understanding of a wide variety of technical fields; now they must add still more. Military commanders will find that, because of the introduction of missiles, leadership and personal skill are more important than ever.

No matter where the soldier, sailor, or airman is working, or what he is doing, his introduction to guided missiles is inevitable. He may serve in a unit or on a ship that has guided missiles as its primary weapons, or that uses them in addition to other armament. Even if his particular unit never has direct contact with these robot devices, its activities will be affected by them. The introduction of these new weapons is forcing new tactics, techniques, logistic plans, and personnel problems on all services. Their importance to the military professional is indisputable.

In addition to the purely combat uses of these weapons, the nonmilitary applications of many mechanisms and techniques now found on guided missiles will eventually be evident. Faster and safer travel on this planet and the exploration of space are by-products of guided-missile development. The solutions to many nonmilitary problems may well be found in missile technology.

But the most immediate problem in missile technology is a

military one. Today, in the midst of this marvelous age of technology, there is no peace. The wars that have erupted in North Africa, the Middle East, Korea, and Indochina are still smoldering, and there is no guarantee that another flare-up will not occur. The tragic slaughter of the Hungarian people, who asked only for freedom, is still fresh in our memories. The rumblings in Africa, Southeast Asia, Latin America, and the Middle East never cease.

The establishment of peaceful freedom has become an obsession with us, particularly those of us who are in uniform, for we know the terrible price of this unending war. We also know by bitter experience in Korea, and by the sharp reminders of Lebanon and Laos, that we must have power, military power, to achieve peace. The means of victory must be held by those who do not want war, if this war is to be ended. This, then, is the primary mission of the nation's armed forces—to provide an overwhelming deterrent to war in its blackest forms, and to furnish the means and assistance to end the gray war.

To establish this objective is easy enough, but to determine how to achieve it is extremely difficult. The United States is faced with the most complex national-security problem in its history, and it is by no means a purely military problem. We all recognize that the permanent steps toward peace and security are political, educational, economic, moral, and spiritual. Military strength is needed to maintain our freedom and to permit these permanent steps to take place. But to correctly intermesh the military gears in the over-all machine is enormously complicated. The primary source of complication is technology, for technological developments are creating a revolution in warfare.

Contemplate the military lessons of the first nuclear decade, the implications of the military actions in Korea, Lebanon, the Formosa Straits, the Congo, and Laos. What is the nature of the military conflict in which we find ourselves? Today's god of war has two faces. With the one face he creates tensions, limited conflicts, and psychological warfare, ever threatening to about-face and show his countenance of total nuclear war. He employs the local *fait accompli*, offers the victory to the accomplished fact of the lightning thrust, the completed mission, the rapid occupation by ground forces, and quick restoration of control. Yet he also emphasizes the prolonged struggle and the war of slow attrition.

This is the military lesson of Korea, Suez, Hungary, Lebanon, Cuba, and Laos. These crises were marked by deadlines measured in hours, with invasions, revolutions, and counterrevolutions developing in a few days. The threat of the conflict expanding into a general war was constantly superimposed on the scene. An unseen guerrilla war still continues in most of these areas.

Our present-day military forces must have a dual capability—that of achieving victory in either a general war or a limited conflict. With a demonstrated capability to wage successfully either an all-out nuclear war or any form of limited war, we have, in conjunction with nonmilitary efforts, the most certain approach to peace itself.

There are those who say that the changes that have come about are evolutionary rather than revolutionary. In a short enough time frame, one might agree; however, if one compares the rate of military change for the past twenty-five years with any period of equal length in the past, revolution becomes a better word.

Only twenty-five years (1935–1960) elapsed from the beginning of a serious missile-development effort until operational missiles in every medium of combat were effective, until the new medium of space had been added, and until warfare itself had been revolutionized (see Appendix A). There have been few changes in recorded military history comparable to the one we are going through today, and there are many indications that it is not over.

2. The New Swords of War

Look in any periodical where missiles are discussed and read such remarks as:

". . . includes a figure of approximately $550 million for ballistic-missile facilities . . .

". . . missile ground-support equipment will cost from $50 million to $75 million . . .

". . . multibillion-dollar missile program . . ,"

Why are such tremendous sums of money being poured into missiles? First, because the development of guided missiles is absolutely necessary, as the pages that follow will show. Second, because, owing to their inherent complexity and radical departure from existing military equipment, development of these new swords of war is expensive. The development time for the U. S. Navy "Bat" missile of World War II, for example, was estimated to be 1000 man-years, and it was almost a simple toy compared to some of today's missiles. These are not glamour weapons fulfilling a dream of push-button warfare that will raise the art of war to some high technical plane. They do not serve the purpose attributed to his branch by a young British cavalry officer who, when asked by the examining board, "What is the purpose of cavalry in war?" replied, "To give tone to what otherwise would be a vulgar brawl!"

Guided missiles have been forced upon us, and to some extent the need has been cumulative. As with other weapons, the existence of one type of guided missile tends to lead to the development of another. It is interesting to note which type first appeared necessary, and how it began the development of a complete family of bullets with brains.

A Definition

First, what is a guided missile? It is a robot device that can be directed to a target by commands originating from outside the weapon or by instruments built into it. To be truly guided, the craft must be capable of changing its course to take account of unpredictable factors or evasive movement of the target. Control devices and propulsion systems used in guided missiles are found in two other types of robot craft as well. The first is an early cousin of the guided missile: the preset missile that can only maintain a predetermined direction, position, or attitude with respect to a fixed reference. The conventional naval torpedo and the German V–1 and V–2 missiles are examples. The second is the remote-controlled pilotless vehicle that is not built for the purpose of attacking a target. Drone aircraft used for reconnaissance and in antiaircraft target practice, and space ships of the future, are examples of this type.

By common usage, the term *guided missile* means a robot craft that flies through the air or space. Actually, no limit should be placed upon the element through which a guided missile moves. It may move in the atmosphere, on land, on or under the surface of the sea, or, theoretically, through the earth. With respect to subearth travel, it is an understatement to say that there are some technical difficulties to be overcome before the "terra-jet" becomes practicable; nevertheless, it has been mentioned by more than one propulsion engineer. However, in speaking of guided missiles one usually means the aerial version.

A guided missile may be classified by type according to the location of the target and the location of the launcher. For example, a controllable bomb launched from an aircraft and destined for a ground or naval target is known as an air-to-surface missile. Similarly, other missiles are designated surface-to-air, surface-to-surface, and air-to-air missiles. These names are abbreviated ASM, SAM, SSM, and AAM, respectively. Other terms are sometimes used as well, new expressions developing quickly in such a dynamic field. For example, surface-to-air missiles are perhaps better known currently as air-defense missiles. The following are other specialized terms that appear in this book:

SRBM—Short-range ballistic missile. An SSM with ballistic-type trajectory and a maximum range of about 62 miles (100 kilometers).

MRBM—Medium-range ballistic missile. An SSM with ballistic-type trajectory and a maximum range of about 950 miles (1500 kilometers).

IRBM—Intermediate-range ballistic missile. An SSM with ballistic-type trajectory and a maximum range of about 1500 miles (2500 kilometers).

ICBM—Intercontinental ballistic missile. An SSM with ballistic-type trajectory and a maximum range of 5000 miles (8000 kilometers) or more.

AICBM—Anti-intercontinental ballistic missile. An SAM designed to counter ICBM's.

ALBM—Air-launched ballistic missile. An ASM with ballistic-type trajectory.

FBM—Fleet ballistic missile. A ship-launched SSM with ballistic-type trajectory.

SLIM (introduced in this book)—Submarine-launched intracontinental missile. A submarine-launched SSM with ballistic-type trajectory, having a maximum range sufficient to reach any target within a continent from adjacent waters, about 1800 miles (3000 kilometers).

STEM (introduced in this book)—Space-to-earth missile. A missile launched from a vehicle in space and directed to a target on earth.

Not as well known, but certainly descriptive, is the jawbreaking German term for guided missile: *das scientifiker geschutenwerkes Firenschpitter!*

The terms *tactical missile* and *strategic missile* are also frequently used to describe shorter- or longer-range ballistic missiles. In this book the two categories are separated at a range corresponding to the maximum required for supporting tactical air-transported troop assaults, about 1000 miles. Thus the SRBM and MRBM are tactical missiles, whereas the IRBM, SLIM, and ICBM are strategic missiles.

Now, how did guided missiles come to be developed? First, airmen sought greater bombing accuracy with less exposure to antiaircraft fire. The ASM came into being to meet this need. Then, to combat modern aircraft (armed with ASM's), vastly improved antiaircraft weapons (SAM's and AAM's) have been essential. With such improved air defense the third development, the SSM, was inevitable. The need for very long-range accurate artillery also pushed the SSM development. Lastly, the existence of the nearly invulnerable surface-to-surface missile (especially the supersonic rocket) forced the further development of a super-SAM, the antimissile guided missile. There are many variations of these types, but fundamentally each is designed because of the continual race between offense and defense. Let us consider each of these missiles in detail.

Air-to-Surface Missiles

When aerial bombing was initiated during World War I, ground and naval forces organized an antiaircraft-artillery defense to oppose it. Airmen, seeking an escape from this antiaircraft fire without loss of bombing accuracy, hit upon the idea of staying above maximum gun range and guiding their bombs after dropping them. The Germans actually accomplished this by dropping from their Zeppelin airships bombs that were electrically controlled by attached wires. Also, in World War II, the first robot weapons to appear in combat were air-to-surface missiles. Thus did the evolution of guided missiles begin.

The need for the air-to-surface missile is even more pressing today. The unacceptable weaknesses of modern high-level bombing are inaccuracy and vulnerability. Accuracy with ordinary bombs can be achieved only by relatively close-in attack of the target—a risky business. If modern air-defense weapons defend the target, attacks will prove prohibitively costly.

The need exists, then, for a bomb that can be released a great distance from the target without sacrifice of accuracy. The air-to-surface missile fills this need.

Surface-to-Air and Air-to-Air Missiles

Because of advances in aircraft, improved bombing techniques, and the development of air-to-surface missiles, gunfire (from the ground or from intercepter aircraft) is inadequate as a defense weapon. Antiaircraft artillery cannot satisfactorily defend a vital target. It cannot cope with the high altitude, speed, and maneuverability of modern bombers. Even if an artillery shell could reach the high-altitude bomber, the time of flight of the shell would be so long that the plane could easily evade the predicted impact point. Artillery can, of course, force bombers to fly so high that their bombing will have greater dispersion; but, because planes may carry nuclear weapons, they must be prevented from bombing at all. Moreover, by launching powered ASM's, bombers can remain at great distances from the target.

The modern high-altitude antiaircraft weapon, the surface-to-air missile, hurtles at the high-flying bomber not only with great speed and range, but with maneuverability as well. As the bomber attempts evasive action, the constantly changing interception point is computed; and the missile, altering its course correspondingly, destroys the target.

This does not mean that all antiaircraft guns will immediately become obsolete. Against low-level, close-in attacks, an accurate, rapid-firing, radar-tracking gun may be effective. However, the engagement range of fixed-trajectory weapons (guns and rockets) is decreasing. Any *unguided* projectile with a time of flight greater than a few seconds is ineffective because the target can maneuver away from the predicted point of interception. In the air defense of strategic targets far from the land battle, SAM's have taken over the gun portion of air defense entirely, and they may take over even in the sudden close engagement with the plane flying at a low altitude.

Not only antiaircraft artillery but also gunfire from intercepter aircraft is in need of augmentation. As sonic velocity is approached and exceeded by both bombers and fighters, aerial gun combat becomes almost impossible. The high-speed fighter has an extremely short time of interception with an enemy bomber and also may have little opportunity to make more than one or two passes. Therefore, because of human limitations, the airman is forced to turn to devices more accurate and responsive than himself. The air-to-air missile is covered in more detail in Chapter 10.

Surface-to-Surface Missiles

Because of the inherent limitations of gun artillery and aircraft, and because of tremendously improved air-defense weapons, the surface-to-surface missile is required. Its purpose is not to pursue some important new target, but to attack already existing targets formerly attacked by cannon artillery or aircraft.

Gun artillery has limited range, lethality, and, at long range, accuracy. Mass-fire techniques do minimize the last two shortcomings, but range is the most important limiting factor. The only solution to greater range is increased size and weight of the gun and even less accuracy. The German "Paris Gun" of World War I is an example of a very long-range gun. It fired a 260-pound shell at a fixed angle of 54° a maximum distance of 80 miles. The high muzzle velocity of 5000 feet per second was so wearing on the barrel that the firing of each shell created a new artillery problem: when fired against Paris, each shell landed about a mile from the preceding shell. Although this gun could be reproduced today, and somewhat bettered, the small improvement would not justify the effort. Artillery as we know it, or with foreseeable improvements, cannot be considered a practical mobile weapon at ranges greater than about 20 miles.

The heavy free rocket (unguided), an important new field-artillery development, greatly increases the lethality and potential range of gun artillery, but it is not accurate at great range. For any unguided projectile there is a range beyond which manufacturing tolerances, variable ambient temperatures, and unpredictable atmospheric conditions preclude reasonable accuracy. The surface-to-surface missile is needed, then, to provide fire against heavily protected targets within artillery range and to extend the effective range of artillery without loss of accuracy.

How about planes? Certainly bombers have extreme range and destructive power, but they have limitations too. First, and most important, a ground target may have so effective an air defense that air attacks will be prohibitively costly. A pilot is faced with two choices. Either he must bomb at extreme altitude and distance from the target, with poor accuracy, or he must descend and bomb while "staring down" the radars of deadly automatic-tracking missiles. Even if he resorts to air-to-surface missiles, the enemy's air-defense missiles still make the pilot's mission extremely dangerous. Second, aircraft may not be available to strike ground targets because of the priority of the air battle. Third, because of weather, aircraft are not always capable of providing the volume and continuity of tactical support that ground forces need. Strategic bombing, too, is hampered by bad weather. Fourth, high-performance aircraft have to be based on large, immobile, vulnerable, and expensive airfields. Finally, the limited accuracy of aircraft bombing should be considered.

This does not mean that the missile will entirely replace the bomber. There will always be a need for piloted combat aircraft, even for conducting strategic nuclear attack. No mechanism can duplicate the ability of the human being to reason and to use good judgment; however, the piloted aircraft will find survival over defended areas increasingly difficult in the missile era.

The Antimissile Missile

With the advent of the intercontinental ballistic missile and the promise of more sophisticated versions to come, there is no choice but to devise a way to stop it. The target will be a hypersonic missile, flying in a high-angle ballistic-type trajectory. Probably it will not be capable of evasive action to avoid interception, but its speed and altitude will make it difficult to locate and destroy. Nevertheless, it must and can be destroyed. It is true that ICBM production plants, storage points, and launching sites can be attacked, but the most certain defense is to intercept the ICBM in flight with another missile.

Problems

It is all very well to argue that we need missiles, but what are the problems involved in using them? For one thing, missile units require considerable logistic support. A rocket-type SSM ready to fire may weigh up to 100 times as much as its own warhead. This means that, for every ton of payload delivered to the enemy, as much as 100 tons of material must be transported to the launching site. In terms of tonnage, the firing of many guided missiles, in the 100-mile-range category will be like firing large volumes of medium artillery, the gun itself being launched with each round. Yet battlefield supply may be simplified, because the missile can be brought up in light, separate loads, assembled, and fired from rear areas. But because of the fragility of missile components, the difficulty and hazards involved in storage and transportation of fuels, and the complexity of much of the equipment, missile logistics will never be easy.

Production cost must also be taken into consideration. It required about 900 man-hours of German labor to produce the simple V–1 missile and 4000 man-hours to build a V–2 rocket. These are impressive figures for single rounds of ammunition, but not impossible ones. They have long since been far exceeded. While the cost per round may be high, the total expense of destroying a particular target may be less with guided missiles than with any other weapon because of the increased accuracy and lethality of guided missiles. For many targets there is no other choice.

The practical problems of research and development, field testing, production, transportation and storage, training, and reliability of operation all add to the cost. Consider reliability, for example. A guided missile may have from dozens to thousands of components operating in series. The failure of any one means a lost missile. A condenser costing fifty cents can and has caused a multimillion-dollar missile to fail. To assure that condensers do not fail, they are now made with the greatest of care and subjected to painstaking tests and checks to assure the highest possible standards of quality. Extremely high standards mean high costs; for reliability must be achieved.

And reliability can be achieved. The "Nike-Ajax," which has been with us for a decade now, with 4000 practice firings has worked up to a reliability of over 85 percent. Practice firings frequently exceed 90 percent "kills."

The problems are mental as well as technical. We are faced with the challenge not only of preventing another Pearl Harbor, on a nationwide scale, but of preventing another Korea—which is the more likely of the two.

In either form of war the military leader may well find a degree of command responsibility thrust upon him that will be far greater than what was normal during World War II or the Korean War. His unit will often be on its own—at all levels of command. During the dark days of the Bastogne defense of World War II, it was the division commander who experienced the loneliness of battlefield isolation. On quite a few occasions in Korea, platoon and company commanders tasted that loneliness. These were considered abnormal situations in those days; in future conflicts they may well be normal.

To meet this challenge, our minds must remain as flexible as high-grade steel, and this flexibility of mind must be cultivated now. We dare not allow ourselves to become imbued with fixed military doctrine. We must accept nothing as fixed and never forget that tactics and technology are ever changing. The study of military history shows us that blind adherence to accepted military dogma is the greatest single cause of defeat in war.

In these times of technological revolution, adherence to a dogmatic solution could be extremely dangerous. H. L. Mencken once said, "There is always a well-known solution to every problem—neat, plausible, and *wrong*." If we ever become satisfied and complacent with our solutions, and war comes, they could very easily prove to be neat, plausible, and *wrong*. Our incapacity for foresight and for reaction to the unexpected could cause us to be left hopelessly behind.

We have seen that guided missiles are born of utter necessity. Therefore, in spite of all problems, they will be developed. They are adaptable to all types of combat and to all forms of military operations. Their uses are limited only by the knowledge and skill of the technician and by the imagination of the tactician. They will be employed widely in the deadly game of war; to avoid that war, we cannot afford to be second-best in their development.

And we must never forget to what ultimate end we develop our military capabilities—to achieve, in conjunction with diplomatic, economic, moral, and spiritual efforts, a real lasting peace. Winston Churchill is reputed to have remarked once that "it looks as though all these new weapons are going to make peace unavoidable." Indeed, this is our intent.

3. From Wan Hu to von Braun

Of all those persons who have proposed the idea of rocketing themselves into space, the first man who seriously tried to do something about it was perhaps the bravest. The first, according to Chinese history, was a scholar and scientist named Wan Hu. He hit upon the idea of propelling himself with the crude rockets known to the Chinese at that time. So, after lashing several dozen of these "JATO" units to his sedan chair, he proceeded to have all the rockets fired simultaneously. We do not yet know just how successful Wan Hu was, for in the blast that followed he disappeared, and nothing has been heard from him since.

The most recent and well-known would-be space traveler is Wernher von Braun, who is notable for his development of the German V–2 rocket. He likewise suggests that if several dozen rocket motors were properly lashed together, this time to his three-stage missile airframe, he could "blast off" into space, never to return until so inclined. Dr. von Braun, now director of the Marshall Space Flight Center of the National Aeronautics and Space Administration, appears to be close to his goal with the giant "Saturn," a 1,500,000-pound-thrust booster with eight rocket motors. With upper stages this "lash-up" will put 25 tons into orbit.

The previous chapter showed why we need guided missiles in modern warfare. It is much more difficult, however, to appreciate how high up the development ladder missile specialists have climbed, and how far they have yet to go. Were the Germans so far ahead of the rest of the world in this field? What has the United States accomplished?

To answer these questions, one must first look back half a century. The first real attempts to steer a machine by remote control were made with torpedoes before the turn of the century. In 1897 a torpedo was experimentally controlled in England in the Thames River. A year later Lieutenant Bradley Fiske, U. S. Navy, applied for a patent on a radio-controlled apparatus for torpedoes, but these first devices were not too practical.

Missiles Before World War II

The use of the military airplane in 1914–1918 aroused considerable speculation over the possibilities of remote-control aircraft. Before the war ended, German research had produced a guided bomb controlled by signals (sent through trailing wires connecting launcher and missile) from an operator in the launching craft. Remote-control torpedo boats were also tested by the Germans.

As early as 1916 the United States Navy and the Army Air Corps began a joint study of pilotless aircraft. The first product of their efforts was a propeller-driven plane with a torpedo-shaped fuselage and an unreliable guidance system. By the early twenties, several pilotless flights had been accomplished, but unsolved control problems and lack of funds seriously hampered the efforts of the budding missile-men. An example of some of the headaches involved was the 1923 flight test of the "Wild Goose," a pontoon-mounted remote-control plane. The safety officer, whose responsibility it was to insure that the Wild Goose did not go haywire and strike unintended targets, had no recourse but to chase the missile in an old de Havilland land plane. He had his rear cockpit loaded with bricks to throw into the propeller of the contrivance, should it misbehave. Fortunately, it was not necessary to unleash the brick attack upon the Wild Goose. Far from being even faintly wild, it did well to struggle into the air at all.

A man of unusual vision in these times was the late Colonel George Holloman of Wright Field. Always looking for advancements in aeronautics and automatic devices, he was involved in many technological improvements during the financially lean

This guided missile was developed by Sperry Gyroscope Company for the United States Navy during World War I. (Photograph by Sperry Gyroscope Company.)

years from 1918 to 1940. Holloman Air Developments Center, the guided-missile test range in New Mexico, is named in honor of this man who, having recognized early the need for guided missiles, was so influential in their development before and during the war.

Meanwhile, improved means of propulsion were being investigated. The leader in this work was Robert H. Goddard of Clark University, Worcester, Massachusetts. His mathematical theories and practical tests represented the real beginning of modern rocket research. As early as 1915 he experimented with solid-propellant rockets. His mathematical study, *A Method of Reaching Extreme Altitude,* was published in 1919. In 1926 he successfully fired the first liquid-fueled rocket motor, and four years later one of his rockets reached a record altitude of 2000 feet and a velocity of 500 miles per hour. He developed the first automatic gyroscopic missile stabilization; he was the first to use vanes in the exhaust stream for steering and the first to fire a rocket at supersonic speed.

Goddard made his findings available to all, but the only nation that took full advantage of the information was Germany. Even so, the Germans were unable to fire a liquid-fueled rocket successfully until 1931.

Originally, there was nothing warlike in the intentions of these men—German or American. Hermann Oberth, the German professor who pioneered rocket development in Europe, was primarily interested in space travel. One of his proposals was a mail rocket for overseas postal service. When he learned of Goddard's 1919 study, he wrote the American this letter:

Dear Sir:

Already many years I work at the problem to pass over the atmosphere of our earth by means of a rocket. When I was now publishing the result of my examinations and calculations, I learned by the newspaper, that I am not alone in my inquiries and that you, dear Sir, have already done much important works at the sphere. In spite of my efforts, I did not succeed in getting your books about this object. Therefore, I beg you, dear Sir, to let them have me. At once after coming out of my work I will be honored to send it to you, for I think that only by common work of the scholars of all nations can be solved this great problem.

> Yours very truly,
> HERMANN OBERTH
> Student Math. Heidelberg

Oberth kept his word and published his 1923 report, *By Rocket to Planetary Space.* Thus were ideas freely exchanged until the power of Hitler became absolute.

Oberth's experiments and publications aroused considerable European interest in rockets. In 1927 a group of German amateur rocket enthusiasts founded a spaceship travel club. They conducted rocket experiments and published a monthly magazine. Public enthusiasm reached new heights when an Austrian aeronautical engineer, Eugen Saenger, published an outstanding book in 1933 called *Rocket Flight Technique.*

German military leaders, now under Hitler, had not forgotten the early attempts to guide bombs during the First World War. The German Army became interested in the activities of the rocket society, and assumed control of the tests. In 1931 the rocket experiments were classified secret and placed under the supervision of Captain Walter Dornberger. The members of the amateur spaceship club were obliged to quit and turn over their patents to the German Government or go to work for the Army (if they were good enough). A nineteen-year-old engineer named Wernher von Braun was among the group who chose to go to work for the Army. He was soon put in charge of the rocket experiments because of his energetic nature and outstanding ability. Although his main interest was—and is today—space travel, he concentrated on the development of military rockets.

After the German Army made a special study of the potentialities of guided missiles in 1933, it built a rocket and guided-missile research center at Peenemünde, a remote section of Germany on the Baltic Sea. This center began fundamental research in every field that might contribute to a solution of guided-missile problems.

Hermann Göring, head of the German Air Force, established a separate rocket research center at Trauen in 1935. It was lavishly equipped for liquid-fuel rocket experiments. He placed the Austrian Saenger at the head of the project and authorized a ten-year research program. Saenger undertook a long-range scientific approach to the problem, aiming at a rocket motor with a 100-ton thrust, four times that of the now-famed V–2.

The most remarkable feature of these two German research centers was that neither knew anything of the other's work. Göring's attitude toward the Peenemünde project was one of jealous rivalry. This uncontrolled interservice competition was a contributing factor to German defeat. The error has been well noted by the United States Department of Defense, which has established over-all control to coordinate all military technology.

The offensive (as opposed to defensive) use of guided missiles received early attention. Because Hitler was determined to engage in aggression and expansion, the Germans developed and used operationally surface-to-surface missiles such as the V–1 and V–2 (to be considered in some detail later). But during the war the growing strength of Allied air power caused the Germans to put heavier emphasis on antiaircraft missiles.

In contrast to the intensified guided-missile research in Germany prior to 1939, little more than preliminary study was done in the United States. In 1932 the American Rocket Society established itself, and it developed a number of different types of rocket motors as early as 1934. A few of the Society's members started a company in New Jersey, Reaction Motors, Inc. The activities of this company greatly benefited missile development during and after the war. Its most recent contribution was the power plant of the supersonic plane, the XS–1. But the World War II air strategy of the United States was based mainly upon long-range bombing with high-performance piloted bombers. This strategy proved to be sound, though the timing was close. Before the end of the war, the need for several types of guided missiles became apparent.

In 1936 the United States Navy began work on a radio-controlled pilotless aircraft to be used as a target in gunnery training. The project was successful and resulted in experimentation with remote-controlled bombs and gliders. This work on the part of the Navy, plus similar target "drone" experiments by the Army (including the Army Air Corps), represented most of the United States' prewar guided-missile research and development. But in 1940, when the Army Air Corps officially established its guided-missile program, Colonel Holloman was placed in charge, and missile development began to move.

Thus, it can now be seen why the Germans entered the war far ahead of the Allies in the development of guided missiles. The German advantage was not determined solely by superior scientific genius, as is commonly believed, but by six years—1933 to 1939—of organized research and development before the war.

Germany's V–Weapons

Germany was able to develop guided missiles in time to mass produce and employ them in significant numbers against the Allies. But the only two weapons that that nation used on a truly large scale were the V–1 "buzz bomb" and the V–2 rocket.

The V–2, a 200-mile-range war rocket, is the most outstanding product of the German effort. Designated the A–4 (rather than V–2) by its designers, it was one of a related series of at least fourteen different missiles built or projected by the technicians at the German Army research center at Peenemünde. Led by von Braun, the Germans built and test-fired the A–1, the A–2, and the A–3. The knowledge gained in building these smaller test missiles was incorporated into the V–2. It is said that by 1939 more than a third of Germany's entire aerodynamic and technological research was devoted to this project.

But from the time World War II began until Germany's collapse, the superrocket development program was subjected to harassments. The two principal causes of trouble were Allied bombers and Hitler, and it is difficult to decide which hampered the V–2 development effort more. First, at the outset of the conflict, Hitler drastically reduced the funds and personnel available to Peenemünde. He assumed that the war would be won before the rockets could be developed.

Despite the setback, early in 1942 the German Army unfolded a plan to Hitler for launching 5000 V–2's a year against England. Hitler's retort was that he wanted a simultaneous assault of 5000 rockets, but, being forced to compromise for practical reasons, he eventually settled on a lesser scheme of 1000 missiles per 24-hour period. But even that goal was never realized.

A desperate race developed to be ready before the Allies attempted to invade Europe. Bombardment was to begin in mid-1943. But in March of that year the plan received a second blow. Mass production was about to begin, troops were training, and tactical plans were being completed, when one restless night *der Führer* dreamed that no V–2 would ever strike England. Refusing to believe, as any self-respecting Scrooge ought to, that the wild nightmare was possibly caused by "a bit of undigested beef," he summarily discontinued the whole program. It took two months of pleading to change Hitler's mind, and August arrived before work was completely resumed. From the German point of view this was possibly the most tragic delay of the entire war.

Not to be outdone by Hitler in delaying the rocket-research

program, the British Royal Air Force bombed Peenemünde on August 17th. Although the research center was severely damaged, the most important effect of the raid was the time consumed by the Germans in dispersing much of their work to other parts of Germany.

It is possible that the development phase of the V–2 program would have been largely completed by August and that the British raid would have affected production but little if Hitler had not interfered the previous March. The earlier production of V–2's and the extra tactical experience that would have been gained by the Germans probably would have resulted in large-scale bombardment of the Southampton port area, where the cross-channel movement originated, and the Normandy beachhead as well. It is doubtful that the Allied operation could have succeeded had the Germans been ready. But the total resultant delay caused by Hitler's dream prevented the V–2 counter-attack from coming until too late.

Hitler again interfered unwisely by insisting that elaborate concrete launching sites be built. The huge emplacements were the exact opposite of the small, mobile launchers recommended by the Army. But the military principles of mobility and surprise were not nearly so important to the dictator as the dramatic effect of concrete fortresses spouting 14-ton rockets. The first permanent sites built were soon located by Allied photo-reconnaissance and repeatedly bombed until useless.

In a frantic race against time the Germans continued their preparations and altered their techniques and equipment to permit mobility of launching sites, but they were too late. June 6, 1944 arrived, and the Allies swarmed across the channel to Normandy. Not until September 1944 did the first rounds "fire for pay," but by then Germany's defeat was inevitable.

The greatest limitation of the weapon was its lack of accuracy. Malfunctions caused many rounds to go awry; but even when the missile functioned perfectly, only about half of the missiles fell within 8 miles of the target center. However, against large area targets such as London and Antwerp the V–2 caused much destruction. There was no effective countermeasure against this supersonic destroyer. Interception in flight by any means was impossible. Launching sites were often changed and, being small, were easy to conceal. Despite Allied superiority in the air, more than 4000 V–2 rockets were fired before the launching areas were physically overrun by our troops.

The V–2 could deliver a ton of high explosives 200 miles in 5 minutes, no small feat even today. This 14-ton monster was 46 feet long and 5 feet in diameter. The remarkable power plant, fed by a highly efficient fuel pump, consumed 9 tons of alcohol and liquid oxygen in 1 minute. At the end of that minute the rocket was traveling a mile per second. Thereafter, it "coasted" in a ballistic trajectory similar to that of an artillery projectile.

When fired at a distant target, the V–2 climbed vertically for 4 seconds and then began to turn in the direction of the target. At approximately 47° from the vertical, the automatic pilot held the missile at that angle of climb until either the motor was shut off or the fuel was exhausted. The range of the missile depended upon the burning time of the motor.

Both militarily and scientifically this rocket was a remarkable weapon. Its existence was proof that Germany was about ten years ahead of the rest of the world in rocket research. The paradox of this missile is that a significant part of the background of knowledge essential for its development came from an American, Dr. Goddard, whose work several years earlier was relatively unnoticed in this country.

But the V–2, to Dr. von Braun, was only the first step toward his ultimate goal—a man-made satellite, or "space station." The next major step was the A–9, essentially a V–2 with large swept-back wings to give it extra gliding range. The third step, the A–10, was to be an 85-ton booster rocket attached to the stern of the A–9. This combination would have a total range of 3500 miles. The final missile of the series was to be the three-stage rocket which, if ever built, would make space travel a reality. By the end of the war, however, the only missile in the series that had reached the "hardware" stage was the V–2.

The other missile fired by the Germans in great quantity was the V–1 "buzz bomb," so nicknamed because of its peculiar noise in flight. A German Air Force weapon, its official designation was FZG–76. It is said that the V–1 came into existence because of interservice rivalry and the Army's early difficulties with the V–2. When Göring, chief of the German Air Force, already envious of the Army's guided-missile progress, first witnessed the firing of a V–2, it failed to leave the platform and instead burned where it stood. The second and third missiles fired for his benefit also failed, exploding violently at the launching point. After these dismal displays Göring remarked that he was now convinced that the V–2 rocket could admirably accomplish short-range destruction! Since Peenemünde was doing so poorly (in his opinion), Göring saw no need for continuing his competition at the Trauen rocket-research center and abruptly closed it. When the plump air marshal finally did see a V–2 launched successfully in 1944, he roared, "This is colossal! We must fire one at the first Nuremberg postwar party rally."

So after these earlier rocket failures the German Air Force concentrated on the development of an entirely different type of missile—the V–1. It was an automatically controlled midwing monoplane powered by a pulse-jet motor. In contrast to the costly and complex V–2, the V–1 was inexpensive, required little time to produce, and used easily obtainable materials. It flew a level, powered flight at an altitude of 1000 to 4000 feet until it dived into the target. The 1-ton warhead could be carried, at about 400 miles per hour, a maximum distance of 160 miles. The weapon's total weight was only about 2½ tons, in contrast to the 14-ton weight of the V–2. Its accuracy was roughly the same as that of the V–2, but, because of the relatively low impact velocity, the burst of the V–1 was often more effective. The V–2 warhead, striking the ground at 1700 to 2500 feet per second, penetrated deeply before exploding, thus expending much of its energy merely to produce a deep hole.

Because of the simplicity of construction and employment of the V–1 missiles, the Germans used them by the thousands. They launched over 5000 missiles against London alone (less than half arrived), resulting in 5500 deaths and the total destruction of more than 23,000 buildings. Despite the ease with which they were shot down, the V–1's were tragically effective. Even the countermeasures themselves, though accounting for roughly half of the "buzz bombs" fired, were extremely costly. One report indicated that the cost to the Allies in man-hours of all countermeasures, production losses, damage repairs, and absenteeism, was almost four times as great as the man-hour cost of the entire V–1 program to the Germans. In bombing launching sites alone, nearly 1500 Allied fliers lost their lives. Yet V–1 attacks were never halted until the launching areas were overrun by Allied troops.

German Surface-to-Air Missiles

As the V–weapon development program continued, steadily increasing Allied bombing of the German homeland forced greater emphasis on the surface-to-air missiles. The search for a satisfactory antiaircraft defense resulted in a desperate development program in which, at one point, more than forty different antiaircraft missile designs were under consideration. But of all these projects, only four showed real promise by the war's end. Fortunately for the Allies, all four projects were too late. The missiles planned were these:

The *"Enzian"* (Gentian). A radio-controlled rocket carrying nearly a half-ton of high explosive, it was intended for heavy bomber formations.

The *"Schmetterling"* (Butterfly). Also a radio-controlled rocket, it was in mass production at the war's end.

The *"Rheintochter"* (Daughter of the Rhine). This rocket was to have a maximum speed of more than 1000 miles per hour. Carrying 330 pounds of explosive as high as 48,000 feet, it would be detonated by a proximity fuse.

The *"Wasserfall"* (Waterfall). This missile came dangerously close to mass employment against our heavy bombers. A 26-foot rocket, it was easy to mass produce and had excellent performance characteristics besides. The *Wasserfall* project had the highest priority of all the surface-to-air missiles projects in Germany.

Other German Missile Projects

In addition to the surface-to-air missiles and V–weapons in Germany's guided-missile program, several air-to-surface weapons were devised. Principally designed for naval targets, these missiles were the first to appear in combat. The two of most practical value were the "Henschel 293" and the "Fritz X." The latter, an armor-piercing radio-controlled bomb, proved its effectiveness against Allied ships at Salerno.

Some work was also initiated on air-to-air missiles. The only missile of note in this field was the "Henschel 298." It was a small rocket that was controlled by either a trailing wire or radio.

As we have seen, Germany's original lead in guided missiles was due to early recognition of their potential value by her leaders. But the greatest incentive for the development of these weapons was Germany's loss of air superiority over Europe. The priority of guided-missile projects was so high that probably at least a third of all German aerodynamic research was in that field.

America's Wartime Missiles

In the United States, there was no urgent necessity for large-scale wartime guided-missile research and development. In 1940 the Air Force established its guided-missile program by starting several guided-bomb (air-to-surface missile) projects. Among the first operational weapons were the "Azon" and the "Razon." These were bombs which could be remotely controlled in azimuth (direction) and in range and azimuth, respectively. However, the requirement that the operator in the parent aircraft be able to see both the bomb and the target until impact severely restricted the use of these missiles. The Azon saw action in both Europe and Burma. It was in Burma, where the ability of the Azon to hit long narrow bridges was demonstrated, that the missile proved its true worth.

The GB–1 was another ASM to see action, this time on German targets. It was a glide bomb with a 12-foot wing and twin tail that automatically maintained its attitude in flight as it glided 20 miles to the target. The obvious advantage of the GB–1 was that the launching plane could drop it out of range of the enemy's antiaircraft defense. In mid-1943, in a single attack on Cologne, 54 B–17's dropped 108 GB–1's and turned back for England without ever coming within antiaircraft-artillery range.

A translation of the German news release of this ASM raid reads:

A high-altitude attack by American bombers against Cologne has been turned back by the fierce antiaircraft fire defending the city, and no bombs were dropped. The accompanying fighter cover, however, composed of small and exceedingly fast twin-tailed aircraft, came over the city at low altitude in a strafing attack. So good were the defenses that every single fighter was shot down; much damage was done by these falling aircraft, all of which exploded violently.

The explosions of the "falling aircraft" was understandably violent, for each was a 2000-pound demolition bomb.

Another outstanding glide bomb was the "Bat." Originally an Air Force project, it was soon transferred to the Navy when its value against naval targets was recognized. The Bat had a radar homing head which enabled it to "see" the target. An operator in the launching plane first "locked" the radar on the target and then released the missile. With a glide ratio of about six to one, the Bat had a range of 10 to 15 miles. Because of hurried and incomplete operator training, the Bat was not particularly successful in combat. Subsequent test, however, have proved this ASM a potent killer of surface shipping. The obvious lesson here is that missiles must have men—trained men—to be effective.

The only SSM built in quantity during the war was a "Chinese copy" of the V–1. The Army Air Corps organized a special squadron to employ the American version, designated the JB–2, but the war ended before the unit could get into action.

The closest thing to a purely American SSM to be used in action was the "Weary Willie." This was an old B–17 loaded with 10 tons of high explosives and flown into a target by remote control. Only a few such "missiles" were employed. But one in particular was flown into military installations at Helgoland, with the resulting destruction of an estimated square mile of critical war materials and building.

The Five Crucial Postwar Years

By the end of the Second World War the Germans had worked on about 140 different guided-missile projects. Had the war continued only a few more months, its final end might have been drastically delayed by German guided missiles.

But the war did end, and there in German laboratories and factories was concentrated the greatest mass of technical knowledge of guided missiles in the world.

Originally, the four occupying powers attempted a cooperative study of German technological developments; but almost immediately they dropped the idea, for Russian plans for exploitation of German technology did not include cooperation with any other nation. American, British, and French investigators did continue to collaborate, however.

The implications were clear. The technologies of the German V–2 rocket, British radar, and the United States' nuclear weapon would some day be combined to produce a new form of artillery that would dominate any conflict in which it was used.

The U. S. military services saw before them a long-range research and development program that would have to be conducted in an atmosphere of postwar peace and by a nation rightly sick of war. The foreign issues of the day were war-damage reconstruction, war-crimes trials, establishment of the United Nations, and efforts to gain Russian cooperation. The important home issues were demobilization and readjustment to a peacetime economy. It was certainly no time to propose an expedited missile program. Thus began five fateful years that did not change in character until the Russian-supported Communists of North Korea attacked South Korea.

One important facet of the postwar missile program was the advantage taken of German wartime progress. To this end Project Paperclip was established. Under this program hundreds of German scientists and technicians voluntarily came to the United States under contract for a probationary period of six months. A number chose to stay and later became U. S. citizens. Unfortunately, Project Paperclip was not always well received by the

Americans. Nazi atrocities were fresh in people's minds, and German scientists were too often referred to as Nazi criminals. This resistance tended to keep the program on a modest scale.

Insofar as national defense is concerned, Project Paperclip is perhaps the least publicized and least expensive, but most important, single program this country has undertaken since World War II. The project permitted the United States to begin with the V–2 rocket engine as a point of departure and go on to develop the rocket engines found fifteen years later in the "Thor," "Jupiter," "Atlas," and "Titan." The United States was able to begin an upper-atmospheric research program almost immediately and with little cost because the Germans, with V–2 rockets brought over for the purpose, were able to provide vehicles to carry aloft the high-altitude instruments. German research in jet propulsion, supersonic aerodynamics, and missile guidance provided points of departure for further research.

Use of the V–2's alone gained several years for America in upper atmospheric research. Of course, the newly formed German-American team did have some problems with the old V–2's. For example, before safety devices were as reliable as they are now, one V–2 rocket fired in 1948 at the White Sands Missile Range in New Mexico went south instead of north and landed in Mexico near Juarez; still, without Project Paperclip, the United States would have needed six to eight years to duplicate German missile technology.

The Germans who were sent to this country under Project Paperclip came as volunteers. They were carefully screened to determine their real scientific value and also had to have no affiliation with war crimes or other adverse Nazi activities. Lastly, assurance was necessary that their absence would have no ill effect on the struggling postwar German economy. They were then offered a maximum of ten dollars a day, plus per diem, for a six-month probationary period. After this period many stayed on to become valuable citizens.

The most famous group under this program, and one of the first to arrive in the United States, was the V–2 rocket-development team led by Wernher von Braun. In the summer of 1945 they assembled with their families near Munich in a housing area set up by the U. S. Army. After the necessary screening processes and arrangements for shipment of rockets, spare parts, and technical papers, the V–2 team, 82 strong, left its families to follow later and departed for Fort Bliss, Texas. Under a lean budget they set up shop in the dusty remains of a former temporary hospital area. The wooden buildings contained no laboratories or equipment but they were the best that could be provided at the time. At least it was a place to begin, and it was close to the new missile firing range at White Sands, New Mexico. Here they assisted in the firing of V–2 rockets in the upper-atmospheric research program and also started a long-range missile project known as Hermes II.

Many missile "firsts" were accomplished with the V–2's. In 1947 the team launched a V–2 rocket from the carrier *Midway* and also successfully carried a monkey in a V–2. On February 24, 1949, with the assistance of the V–2 group, the Army successfully fired a two-stage rocket to a record-breaking altitude of 250 miles. This was a V–2 with a smaller missile nicknamed "Wac Corporal" attached to its nose. When the V–2 reached a predetermined height, the Wac Corporal separated from it and accelerated to a maximum speed of 5000 miles per hour. This was man's first penetration of space and first large multistage rocket. Altogether, 69 V–2 rockets were fired in support of Army, Navy, and Air Force research activities.

In 1949 the U. S. Army established Redstone Arsenal, Alabama, as its major missile-development center. The V–2 group moved there later to become the nucleus of the Army Ballistic Missile Agency and eventually to join the National Aeronautics and Space Administration.

During this period of initial German assistance, the United States launched several independent missile-development programs. In February 1945 the Army contracted with Bell Telephone Laboratories and Western Electric Company to initiate an air-defense missile program. This was the beginning of the now-familiar family of "Nike" missiles. The Jet Propulsion Laboratory of the California Institute of Technology began its famous series of missile developments nicknamed "Private," "Corporal," and "Wac Corporal," which finally culminated in the "Sergeant" in 1960.

White Sands Proving Ground (now White Sands Missile Range) was established in July 1945, and in October the first Army missile battalion was activated there. This range was the first of three national missile ranges, each managed by a different military service but available for use by all services. In 1947 the Antiaircraft and Guided-Missile School was so designated at Fort Bliss, and a joint Army-Navy guided-missile department was established.

The experimental firing of a V-2 rocket from the *Midway* demonstrated the vast new possibilities of naval warfare. Soon after World War II, the Navy converted the *USS Norton Sound*, formerly a seaplane tender, into a guided-missile ship for experimental firing. The Navy established a research center at the Applied Physics Laboratory, Johns Hopkins University, and in California founded two important guided-missile centers. On a sandspit at Point Mugu, California, a band of curious and friendly seals found their favorite sunning spots converted into a missile test-firing and training range. Established on October 1, 1946, it is now known as the Pacific Missile Range, the second of the three national missile ranges. To the east, in the California desert near Inyokern, the Navy Bureau of Ordnance built a research and development center for rockets, guided missiles, aviation, and underwater ordnance. Known as the Naval Ordnance Test Station, this installation is today largely responsible for many U. S. Navy missile successes.

During this early postwar period the Navy concentrated on air-defense and air-to-surface missiles. The *"Kamikaze"* (manned-missile) threat at Leyte Gulf and off Okinawa had been extremely serious. Profoundly impressed with this form of attack, the Navy emphasized air-to-surface missiles to attack shipping, and air-defense missiles on shipboard to counter such weapons in the hands of an enemy. The Navy at this time also began development of the "Viking" and "Aerobee" high-altitude research vehicles. By 1947 the Navy was actively pursuing development of all types of missiles. Out of these early years of effort came the "Regulus," "Terrier," "Talos," and other missiles in today's U. S. naval arsenal of weapons.

The Air Force, a separate service by 1947, first concentrated on air-launched missiles and long-range pilotless-aircraft-type missiles. Today's "Snark" and "Matador," pilotless bombers, are products of that era. With such weapons under development it was obvious that a long-range proving ground was needed. So, on October 1, 1949, at Cape Canaveral, Florida, the Air Force established a test range that now extends to the southeast more than 6000 miles. It is presently known as the Atlantic Missile Range and is the third of the three national missile ranges. Here the first Air Force guided-missile squadron was formed. Designated the First Pilotless Bomber Squadron (Light), it employed the Matador, a turbojet-powered SSM.

It was during this crucial postwar period that a fateful decision was made leading to the present U. S. lag in the big space boosters. The decision was to depend upon aircraft rather than missiles for strategic delivery of nuclear weapons. Intercontinental ballistic missiles appeared to be far off, as indeed they were, and nuclear weapons were too large to be put in missiles that would be operational in the near future. So the decision was made to continue to deliver nuclear weapons as bombs in large aircraft.

Such a decision can hardly be criticized, for it resulted in giving the United States a significant intercontinental nuclear capability in the shortest possible time. Since this country would not initiate a nuclear war unless attacked, there was no choice but to be ready as soon as possible. To wait for a better delivery system was not acceptable. However, this decision removed any urgency from the development of large missiles capable of great range and payload capacity.

In Russia the five fateful postwar years were handled quite differently. In contrast to the U. S. policy of conducting a relatively small missile-research program pointed toward operational systems five to ten years hence and of utilizing German technology with propriety, the Soviet Union emphasized immediate development of operational systems and ruthlessly exploited German technology in order to accomplish this goal.

Rocketry was not new to the Russians. Serious Russian interest in rockets and space travel was shown as far back as the beginning of the twentieth century. The Russian mathematician Konstantin Tsiolkovski published an article on "The Principles of Rocket Flight" just after the turn of the century. In 1903 he published a paper entitled "Investigation of Universal Space by Means of Rocket Flight." He also built rocket models but apparently never launched them.

The tremendous upheaval of World War I and the Russian Revolution prevented much more progress until 1923 when the Soviet Institute of Theoretical Astronomy was founded. Russian interest increased thereafter in both liquid- and solid-propellant rockets. In 1934 the government organized a rocket-research program and in 1935 fired a meteorological rocket to a height of six miles.

During World War II the Russian Army used rocket artillery extensively. Rocket-artillery units often had an elite status and enjoyed use of the best equipment. Some of the Russian rocket artillery in Leipzig in 1945 showed this preferential treatment. The rocket launchers were mounted on new lend-lease Studebaker trucks in contrast to the thousands of horse-drawn gun-artillery units. The equipment was in good condition and the soldiers were well dressed and well disciplined.

The Russians were keenly interested in the German V–2 rocket and in other modern military developments, and immediately after the war initiated a major military development program. It is obvious in retrospect that the Soviet Union was pointing toward a new modern military capability in as short a time as possible. In spite of the compelling requirement for extensive reconstruction of war-damaged areas, a huge army of at least 150 divisions was retained and modernized. The modernization program gave high priority to the development of ballistic missiles and nuclear warheads, and by 1950 the Soviet Army had both. Thus in 1950 the Russian nation was a nuclear power with which to reckon. The Korean War of 1950 and subsequent cold- and limited-war actions could then be pursued with relative impunity.

The Russian postwar exploitation of German technology was swift. The Soviet Union seized all the missiles, production plants, development centers, and scientists in East Germany that could be of any benefit. Voluntary recruitment of the Germans was tried at first but failed because of German fear of the Russians. The Russians then resorted to kidnapping—at first in small numbers and then in mass. According to former Russian Lieutenant Colonel Vladimir Shabinsky, who fled from Russia in 1947, the Soviets kidnapped more than 2000 German scientists and technicians. The largest part of this forced transfer to Russia occurred in a single night in October 1946. Throughout East Germany selected people were awakened, loaded on trucks with their families and household goods, and by morning found themselves on trains bound for Russia. There is no evidence that Nazi affiliations or concern for the German economy affected their choices.

Peenemünde, the German rocket test center, was reactivated and put to work on advanced V–2's. Apparently the goal was to pursue a development program to increase the range and accuracy of the basic missile and put it into production as soon as possible. By 1950 the underground Mittelwerk factory at Nordhausen, which had a wartime capacity of 900 V–2's per month, was again in production.

The Soviets also pressed for an early air-defense capability with missiles. Improved versions of the German *Rheintochter* and *Wasserfall* were put into service in the defense of Moscow.

The Soviets initiated a long-range development program as well. Their missile and space achievements of the late 1950's and early 1960's are products of this program. It is also apparent that the Soviets went directly to work on an intercontinental ballistic

missile to carry their earlier nuclear warheads. The first-generation warheads were undoubtedly large; hence the carriers had to
be large. The result was a 1,300,000-pound thrust booster that
gave the Soviet Union its dramatic lead in space exploration in
the late 1950's.

In retrospect, the contrast of major Soviet activity to the
relatively modest efforts of the United States may be somewhat
shocking. During these five years America was spending annually
about 1 percent of the money on missiles that it was spending in
1960. It was a period of financially lean years for missile work,
created in part by public revulsion for war. Another reason for
the low expenditures was the decision to go into basic research
(the low-cost period of a development effort) pointed toward
sophisticated missile systems in the future, rather than immediate
and costly production of weapons of marginal value. "Conventional" weapons were relied upon for the near future.

But there is no avoiding the unpleasant truth that greater
effort should have been made during those first five years and
that the 1945–1950 doldrums are in great part responsible for the
lack of a clear-cut United States superiority in missiles and space
in the 1960's. As von Braun put it, "Our present dilemma is not
due to the fact that we are not working hard enough now, but
that we did not work hard enough the first six to ten years after
the war."

The Aspirin Age

One might well identify the 1950–1957 period with a label
similar to that of other times. Previously there had been the Air
Age, the Atomic Age, and the Jet Age. The seven-year period
was too soon for the Space Age; that age began with *"Sputnik I."*
The period could be identified as the Age of Scientific Acceleration; for it was certainly that, though not uniquely. Perhaps in
view of the headaches of the period, we should call it the Aspirin
Age.

The first big headache began abruptly in Korea and it has not
yet subsided. The first Communist rifle shot across the thirty-

eighth parallel in Korea in July 1950 was no doubt aimed at a South Korean soldier, but its most important casualty was the policy of extreme military economy in the United States. The five lean years came to an abrupt end. No one knew what the Korean War would lead to—World War III being a distinct possibility—but nearly everyone agreed that, short of world disarmament, the United States must never again be found in a state of military weakness.

A succinct example of the change of attitude can be seen in the missile budget. From 1945 to 1950 the missile program in this country averaged about $70 million a year, gradually creeping up to $135 million by 1950. The first year of Korea saw $800 million spent on missiles, and the second more than $1 billion. The missile budget steadily increased until in fiscal 1960 $7 billion was allocated to missiles. Thus the United States is currently spending 100 times the money it did in pre-Korea days.

With the impetus of the Korean War, Secretary of Defense George C. Marshall, famous Army Chief of Staff of World War II, established a director of guided missiles in his office. Through this office wartime decisions came in rapid succession to "weaponize" selected missiles that showed promise of early solution. The "Honest John," "Corporal," "Nike-Ajax," "Matador," and "Terrier" received the nod at this time, and within a few years all were operational. By 1951 the Nike-Ajax had successfully accomplished the world's first interception of an aircraft by a missile.

It was also during these early days of the Korean War that the development of a fusion-type nuclear warhead was assured. Not only headaches, but soulsearching followed the discovery, for there appeared to be no limit to the magnitude of this horrible weapon. The United States could not afford to be without fusion weapons if other nations could produce them as well; so the development program began.

Since it appeared that a fusion warhead could be made small enough to be carried in a large (100,000-pound thrust) rocket, the Army began development of the "Redstone" missile. The program proceeded rapidly. In 1952 the Atomic Energy Commission detonated the first fusion warhead, and in 1953 the Army launched the first Redstone missile. By this time it was evident that fusion warheads could be made a fraction of the size and weight of the warhead intended for the Redstone. This breakthrough had two profound effects. First, with propulsion and guidance systems then on hand or nearly developed, missiles with thousands of miles of range became feasible. The second and unintended effect was to postpone for at least five years the development of a booster in the 1,000,000-pound class. Such a booster would be needed for space systems, not missilery; but space exploitation was not then an objective. This lack of large space boosters later had the effect of extending the Aspirin Age into the Space Age.

The U. S. Air Force saw in this warhead breakthrough truly feasible intercontinental-range artillery. The "Atlas" missile program received new impetus. To supervise this and other Air Force ballistic-missile projects, the Air Force established the Ballistic Missile Division in 1954 under its Air Research and Development Command and placed Major General Bernard Schriever in command. Under this new organization the Atlas and Thor ballistic missiles began to take shape and within five years were operational.

Progress was evident in all missile activities. By the end of 1955 Redstone Arsenal had become one of the major guided-missile facilities of the nation, a scene of feverish activity and accomplishment. It was a $43-million investment including a huge static test stand, calibration stand, and a million square feet of floor space in shops, assembly buildings, and laboratories. When the Department of Defense authorized the Army in November to develop the "Jupiter" missile, it was here that the Army Ballistic Missile Agency was established to undertake this project. Made up initially of the German rocket team, the organization grew to more than 4000 scientists, technicians, and military personnel.

The Jupiter project proceeded with the greatest possible speed. In September 1956 a test vehicle known as Jupiter C rose from Cape Canaveral, climbed 700 miles into space, and headed down-range. The huge rocket achieved a velocity of more than 15,000 miles per hour and landed 3000 miles from the launch point. Had an additional rocket stage, which the missile could have carried, been fired to boost the speed a little more, its velocity would have been orbital; the world's first satellite would have been American, more than a year ahead of *Sputnik I*. However, the decision had been made that the first U. S. satellite firing was to be a civilian effort, and a military missile was not to be used.

The year 1956 did see establishment of the first U. S. satellite project, and the race for space was on. It was not recognized in this country as a race, but it was in the Soviet Union. The United States publicly announced that a satellite would be placed in orbit, established a tentative schedule, and went to work.

As a part of this program, responsible authorities decided to build a completely new booster system. Thus was the "Vanguard" project begun—cause for consumption of more aspirin. This decision created a fatal delay in the U. S. satellite program, for extensive new component development was required and a time-consuming "debugging" process had to be undertaken to develop the new booster. The end product was a satisfactory booster that did eventually orbit a small satellite, but after the Soviets had achieved the distinction of being first, and even after the United States had placed two other satellites in orbit with another booster.

A really nagging headache of the period was the growing problem of interservice and intraservice rivalry. In the early 1950's guided-missile technology developed so rapidly that conflicts began to develop between and within the military services. The new weapons rendered the traditional roles of the Army, Navy, and Air Force obsolete and overlapping. They threatened the obsolescence of proven weapon systems within the services, creating heated internal arguments. What was to become of the tank, the airplane, the aircraft carrier? New missile systems had such revolutionary capabilities that the future of these symbols of land, air, and sea power was uncertain. It was a period of controversy and confusion, created in part by conflicts of interest between and within the services, but primarily by the revolutionary changes in warfare. This controversy was as heated in other countries as it was in the United States, though less advertised.

To alleviate the problem, Secretary of Defense Charles E. Wilson in March 1956 appointed a special assistant for guided missiles to coordinate Defense Department missile activities. In order to clarify the missile roles of the services, Mr. Wilson published a memorandum on November 26, 1956, which assigned the following responsibilities:

(1) ICBM's—Air Force

(2) IRBM's—Air Force (land based) and Navy (ship based)

(3) SSM's—Army (up to 200 miles range; studies for missiles of greater range permissible)

(4) Land-based air-defense missiles—Army (local air defense) and Air Force (area air defense)

(5) Ship-based air-defense missiles—Navy.

This directive clarified some responsibilities but was vulnerable to criticism and varying interpretation. The criticisms were that it permitted the development of missile systems without the user being designated, and that it established an artificial 200-mile limit on Army missile artillery (a restriction later relaxed). The directive established a concept of local versus area air defense that had no precise meaning and that was soon rendered technologically obsolete. To further centralize all military technological developments, Secretary Wilson in March 1957 appointed an Assistant Secretary for Research and Engineering, still retaining the assistant for guided missiles. This was the situation when *Sputnik I* was orbited.

The period 1950–1957 was one of progress in all fields of missilery, of emphasis on nuclear and thermonuclear weapons and their long-range delivery by aircraft, of emphasis on defense against aircraft delivery, of confusion with respect to roles and missions of the services, and of frequent organizational changes within the Defense Department to cope with management problems.

The missile revolution was creating even more of a dilemma in the United Kingdom. The British budget simply could not absorb both an aircraft- and a missile-development program. Britain was not only faced with the same strategic problem as the United States, that of having an adequate defense posture at all times, but also with the special problem of living within range of the new Soviet missiles. By this time the British had joined the exclusive nuclear club as a third member, but could afford only one delivery means, either missile or plane.

For several years they wrestled with the problem. Purchase of U. S. aircraft and missiles was considered. Finally the rapid advance of missile technology, proximity of the enemy missile threat and the uselessness of aircraft as a countermeasure, the requirement for a continuously adequate posture, and the increasing pressure of an overextended budget all served to force the government to a bold and dramatic decision—to scrap aircraft in favor of missiles. This decision was the first of its kind by any nation since the missile was conceived.

It was the fourth of April 1957 when Defence Minister Duncan Sandys announced the decision to phase out combat aircraft and turn to missiles. The phasing was to be gradual, but the British fighter command and bomber command were to be eliminated as soon as adequate missile power was available. All further development of bombers and fighters was to be discontinued; except for reconnaissance and transport units, the future Royal Air Force was to be a missile corps. Its strength was to be decreased from 230,000 to 140,000 men over a five-year period as missiles replaced aircraft.

Born of economic necessity and a technological revolution, the decision rocked the military world. In a few months the Soviets would also announce their emphasis on missiles; the trend had been established.

Although public knowledge of the Soviet guided-missile program is extremely limited, one can deduce in retrospect several aspects of their program during this period. From the Korean War to *Sputnik I,* the Soviets apparently concentrated on obtaining a thermonuclear-weapon capability, on an ICBM to deliver it, and on exploration of space. Their program was probably a continuation toward objectives established before the Communist invasion of South Korea. The long-range objective was modernization of the armed forces. A distinct level of modernization was achieved before they allowed the Korean War to be initiated. The next level of modernization has now been achieved, the equipping of Soviet Army units with thermonuclear-tipped ICBM's.

The Soviet Union apparently enjoyed no such technological breakthrough in warhead size in the early 1950's as the United States did. The first fission weapon was burst only as recently as 1949. The first fusion weapon was not detonated until 1955, and it was not a very small device. An intercontinental ballistic missile to carry it had to be correspondingly large, perhaps with a thrust of as much as 700,000 pounds. Thus it is probable that because the Soviets *had* to develop a large missile they achieved as a bonus effect an early space capability. And space exploration was by no means being ignored by the Soviets. It may have been a technological coincidence that big missiles could be used as space boosters, but the coincidence was recognized at once.

The Soviets had conducted vertical rocket flights with animals since 1950. In 1953 they began serious investigations of flight to the moon. In 1955 the government established the Interagency Commission for Interplanetary Communications, and planning for *Sputnik I* began. When in 1956 the United States announced its plan to orbit a satellite, it is obvious that the Soviet schedule was arranged so that *Sputnik I* would be first.

The significant contrast between the American and Russian military development programs from 1950 to 1957 is that the United States emphasized strategic air delivery of nuclear weapons, whereas the Soviet Union emphasized missile delivery. There is little doubt that this country had the superior weapon-delivery capability during these seven years. The United States was forced to maintain a high level of effectiveness throughout the period as a deterrent to Russian attack. The Soviets had no such requirement for a continuous high level of effectiveness, for they were not threatened with attack. They could therefore gamble with little risk on leap-frogging air delivery and concentrating on missile delivery. The Soviets had bombers, but apparently only enough to create an ostensible threat.

In August 1957 Russia triumphantly announced that it had launched the world's first ICBM. Now, the Russian news agency *Tass* indicated, "no part of the earth is too far away; strategic air forces are obsolescent."

Then came *Sputnik I.*

Dawn of the Space Age

On the fourth of October 1957 history was in the making when a huge Russian rocket lifted off its pad and bored up through the heavy atmosphere. High above the earth in the thinning air it began to tip in a northeasterly direction (65° north of east) with ever-increasing speed. Multiple stages dropped off the 185-pound payload until at 600 miles altitude it leveled off at a speed of 16,000 miles per hour. Now, without power or lift in airless space, it began to fall back, but in a circular path whose center was the center of the earth. Ninety-six minutes later it had "fallen" all the way around the earth, yet was still 600 miles above it. *Sputnik I* was in orbit.

The world's first man-made satellite was significant in many respects. Not only was it launched ahead of the first U. S. satellites, the "Explorer I and the "Vanguard"; it outclassed them in other ways. The Russian *Sputnik* (meaning "fellow traveler," not "small potatoes") weighed 185 pounds compared to the Explorer's 31 pounds and the Vanguard's 50 pounds. Furthermore, *Sputnik*'s orbit took little advantage of the free eastward speed given a satellite by the rotation of the earth. And thirdly, the orbit was 600 miles high. To lift such a weight to such a relatively high and difficult orbit, *Sputnik's* first-stage rocket must have produced at least 200,000 pounds of thrust. Vanguard had a 28,000-pound thrust.

The effect on world opinion was immediate and lasting. The dramatic feat convinced many that Soviet Russia was at least equal and probably superior to the United States in missilery. The orbiting satellite was directly equated to military power and, in the minds of many, in a single step the Soviet Union became the top military power on earth.

Other missile-launched space vehicles followed rapidly. On November 3rd, a month after the first satellite, the Russians launched a second. Five days later the U. S. Secretary of Defense ordered the Army to proceed with preparations for launching a satellite to back up the Vanguard effort. This order precipitated a "crash project" (see Appendix B) that culminated on the last day of January 1958 in the launching of "Explorer I," the first American satellite, by a Jupiter C.

Meanwhile, the United States Government was developing an organization for the space effort. Girding itself for military exploitation of space and new scientific advances, the Department of Defense established the Advanced Research Projects Agency (ARPA). While its mission was to direct any advanced research projects the Secretary might designate, the organization was primarily space oriented.

At the same time, a civilian space agency was formed for non-military space development and exploration. On July 29, 1958 the National Advisory Committee for Aeronautics was redesignated the National Aeronautics and Space Administration (NASA). Since initially it had little "space capability," the newly formed NASA was expanded to include some of the most competent and experienced scientists and facilities available. In December 1958 the Army's Jet Propulsion Laboratory was transferred to NASA, and in July 1960 the major part of the Army Ballistic Missile Agency, under the direction of Wernher von Braun, was transferred and designated the Marshall Space Flight Center. Thereby NASA acquired more than 5000 scientists, technicians, and other assistants, nearly thirty years of experience in rocketry, and many millions of dollars worth of facilities.

The space launchings continued. In mid-May of 1958 the Russians launched a third earth satellite weighing 3000 pounds. In January 1959 a powerful missile hurled a Russian space probe past the moon and into orbit around the sun. If the Russian announcement—that the last stage of the vehicle weighed a ton and a half—was accurate, the first-stage thrust had to have been at least 1,000,000 pounds. Two months later the United States followed suit by placing "Pioneer IV" in a solar orbit. Other space exploits followed in swift succession until their existence became almost commonplace. Not until April 12, 1961 did the man on the street, whether in Times Square or Red Square, give a space-shot headline more than a passing glance.

April 12th raised eyebrows because on that day the first human being in the history of the earth left its protective blanket of atmosphere and went into orbit. Russian Major Yuri Gagarin sped northeastward nearly 200 miles above the earth at 18,000 miles per hour until, 89 minutes later, he was again at the point in space where he had started. Meanwhile the earth had rotated eastward some 22½°, so Gagarin had to orbit onward another 20 minutes to catch up with his moving landing point. In 109 minutes he made a 26,000-mile trip around the earth and landed safely. Momentous as this event was, it too soon became just one of several manned adventures into space. United States astronauts Alan B. Shepard, Jr., and Virgil I. Grissom soon made their ballistic space flights, and another Russian, Gherman Titov, made a multiple-orbit space flight. On February 20, 1962 Lieutenant Colonel John H. Glenn, Jr., made the first U. S. manned orbit. His "Friendship 7" circled the earth three times in four and one-half hours. The manned missile was a reality.

But the marriage of missile and space vehicle is destined to be shortlived. Space probers are demanding their own peculiar forms of transport. They want to be able to lift many tons of payload and are willing to accept complicated liquid propellants, vulnerable fixed launching sites (from a military point of view), and long countdowns to do it. The resulting products will not be useful as weapons; the huge multiple-engine Saturn is an example. Modified missiles are serving as the first space transports until the Saturns and others are ready to take over the job.

In May 1961 the President of the United States recommended to the Congress that manned flight to the moon be established as a national goal. The project was assigned to NASA, which plans to accomplish it by 1970. A contract has been awarded for the design, development, and construction of a three-man spacecraft named "Apollo," which is to land men on the moon and return them to earth. The booster-rocket program includes development of a family of three different giant vehicles having first-stage thrusts of 1,500,000 pounds, 7,500,000 pounds, and 12,000,000 pounds.

Enormous facilities are being developed to implement the moon program. A manned-spacecraft center is being established at Houston, Texas. Almost 2,000,000 square feet of manufacturing space at New Orleans, Louisiana are being converted into the largest vehicle-assembly area in the United States. The Saturn and Advanced Saturn space boosters will be assembled there when produced. Furthermore, NASA is acquiring 73,000 acres along the Florida coast adjacent to Cape Canaveral for construction of the moon-launch sites. The principal development activities will be concentrated at the manned-spacecraft center in Houston and at the Marshall Space Flight Center in Huntsville, Alabama.

While their more illustrious peacetime cousins have enjoyed world attention, the missiles of war have continued to advance. Surface-to-surface missiles increased in range, accuracy, simplicity, and lethality. Both the U. S. Atlas and the Russian T–3A ICBM's reached 9000 miles, a third of the way around the earth. The 1961 annual report of the Secretary of Defense stated that thirteen Atlas ICBM squadrons were scheduled to be organized. A second liquid-fueled giant, the two-stage Titan, passed its final tests and stood ready to join the deterrent force, with twelve squadrons scheduled. Refined inertial-guidance systems continued to improve accuracy, and solid propellants greatly simplified procedures and equipment. Warheads grew smaller and more powerful, and in February 1960 a fourth nation, France, demonstrated that it could arm its missiles with nuclear warheads.

New mobility became possible. The U. S. Army "Pershing" project promised a helicopter-transportable missile with eventual MRBM range. The U. S. Navy's solid-propellant missile, "the "Polaris," proved to be so successful that soon five submarines, each carrying sixteen missiles, were operational, with numerous additional submarines scheduled for construction. The U. S. Air Force "Minuteman," a 5500-mile-range solid-propellant ballistic missile, demonstrated its readiness in 1961. As a result, the Department of Defense accelerated its production rate and development of improved range, reliability, and accuracy characteristics. Thus, with the arrival of Atlas, Titan, Polaris, and Minuteman as hardware, not drawing-board concepts, a new deterrent in the form of strategic missile artillery was a reality.

Premier Nikita Khrushchev did not pass up the opportunity to threaten with his own missile deterrent. In July 1960 he warned that "Soviet artillery can hit America if the U. S. moves against Cuba." Thus did Americans find the policy of massive retaliation being threatened by the Soviets. In 1961 the Soviets ushered in the 50- to 100-megaton warhead.

Defensive missiles were not far behind. The U. S. Army "Hawk" missile demonstrated its versatility by intercepting both jet target drones flying at treetop height and short-range ballistic missiles in supersonic flight. The Army "Nike-Hercules" successfully attacked a test target at a height of over 150,000 feet. On another occasion the Nike-Hercules destroyed a target traveling at three times the speed of sound and more than 100,000 feet above the earth; however, the most dramatic test of air-defense weapons to date came on May Day 1960, over Russia. If the Russian announcement is to be believed, a Soviet air-defense artillery unit intercepted American Francis Gary Powers' U-2 aircraft at more than 60,000 feet with a single missile. Quite independent of the international implications of this incident is the sober news that, so far as can be determined, an air-defense missile actually reached and destroyed a high-altitude jet aircraft. May Day 1960 becomes a historic date for several reasons, one of which is that it marked the first successful combat employment of an air-defense missile.

By 1960 the U. S. antimissile missile was beginning to show promise in a third-generation Nike. The feasibility of intercepting shorter-range ballistic missiles had been demonstrated (Nike-Hercules against Corporal) and the first anti-ICBM missile was about to be tested. This defensive giant, the "Nike-Zeus," was

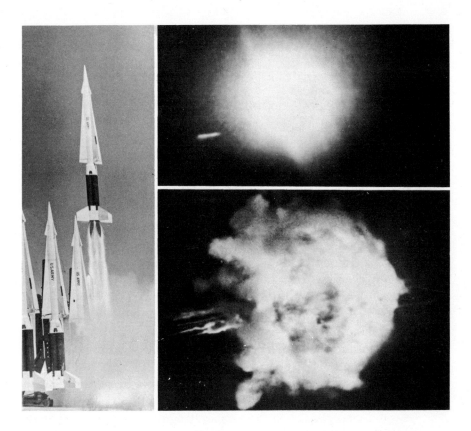

Antimissile missile. The Nike-Hercules shows its ability to "kill" another supersonic high-altitude Hercules. (U. S. Army photograph.)

conceived in studies in the early 1950's, and by 1956 component development and experimental work had begun. Following the scheduled development program, the Army fired several test missiles in 1960 at White Sands Missile Range and planned full-scale tests against the Atlas ICBM as a target. In 1962 the Nike-Zeus successfully intercepted a Nike-Hercules target.

Thus, as with sword and shield, bullet and armor plate, tank gun and antitank gun, the battle of offense versus defense raged in missile developments. The outcome of this battle is not yet evident, but it is clear that mankind had better find other ways than nuclear warfare to settle its differences.

4. How They Fly

The tactical necessity for guided weapons having been established, one might think the military services need only call in the scientists, engineers, and technicians and present them with the military characteristics they want missiles to have. But without a basic understanding of the technology of these weapons, military planners could not possibly make reasonable requests. Moreover, in following missile-development projects they would be unable to differentiate between legitimate technical difficulties and delays born of incompetence. The tactical use of guided missiles in the field requires technical skills as well. Even personnel not directly involved in missile employment can better coordinate their own weapons and effect countermeasures against enemy missiles by appreciating the technical limitations of guided missiles.

Therefore, for a better understanding of missiles, a short technical briefing is in order. Four fields—aerodynamics, guidance, propulsion, and payloads—will be covered. This chapter on missile aerodynamics will introduce to the reader some of the major considerations in missile flight and design.

First, what is the nature of the medium in which a guided missile moves?

The Nature of Air

Of the four basic mediums through which a guided missile might move—air, water, space, and earth—air is the most important and most frequently used. Eventually, space travel and underwater travel may be no less important, and they are certainly not being ignored today, but subearth travel must still be relegated to the unknown.

Both air and water are fluids, and the study of the motion of bodies in fluids is known as fluid mechanics. That branch of fluid mechanics dealing with air in particular is known as aerodynamics. Hydrodynamics is the term usually applied to the study of the motion of bodies in water, although it is often used in the general sense for other fluids as well.

Because the very nature of the medium in which a missile moves affects the shape, speed, and maneuverability of that missile, it is well to know the more important properties of a fluid medium. These are density, compressibility, and viscosity.

Air density is the mass per unit volume of air. The density of air at sea level under standard conditions is about 0.077 pound per cubic foot. The density of water is about 62.4 pounds per cubic foot, more than 800 times that of air. The density of air is dependent upon its temperature and pressure and rapidly decreases with increasing altitude. Air density directly affects missile performance because the moving missile sets a large volume of air in its vicinity into motion. The greater the air density, the greater the inertia, and the more energy the missile expends on the air. The lower density of air is one reason why much higher speeds are possible in air than in water.

Compressibility is the ability of a substance to change volume when placed under pressure. Air has high compressibility, for its volume is easily changed by pressure variation. In contrast, water has very low compressibility. The term *bulk modulus of elasticity,* often used in aerodynamics, is the exact opposite of compressibility. In fact, water is more than 14,000 times as hard to compress as air. For simplicity of analysis, air can be thought of as incompressible for low speeds and low altitudes. However, except for launching, the guided missile usually flies high and fast, and compressibility effects cannot be ignored. On the other hand, water is virtually incompressible no matter what the speed of a body through it. This is why shock waves do not develop in water as they do in air.

Viscosity is that property of a substance which resists shear, that is, the motion of one layer of the substance with relation to the layer next to it. High viscosity means high resistance to relative motion. Heavy molasses, for example, has high viscosity, for it is reluctant to pour out of a container, such action requiring the relative motion of successive layers. Applied to the medium of a missile, the higher the viscosity, the slower the speed of the missile. Water is about 62 times as viscous as air. Once again, for greater missile speed the nod goes to air, though the difference is not so extreme as in the first two properties. For some studies it is possible, without excessive error, to consider air nonviscous. But as before, because of the high speed and altitude of most missiles the more simple theory must be abandoned.

The Atmosphere

The behavior of air under known conditions is quite predictable. If the atmosphere were to lie in a quiet and motionless blanket about the earth, the problem of aerodynamics would be far simpler than it is. But, unfortunately, the atmosphere is most ill-behaved. The density, compressibility, viscosity, and temperature not only vary greatly with altitude but also change constantly. In fact, both compressibility and density are affected by temperature. From sea level up to about 6 miles—within the troposphere—the temperature decreases with increasing altitude, from an average of about 60°F to −67°F. It is within this lowest region that weather disturbances usually originate.

From about 6 miles to 20 miles the temperature of about −67°F is fairly constant. This layer—the stratosphere—is usually thought to have steady, predictable winds, although a Norwegian research group maintains that it has detected intermittent vertical velocities up to 250 miles per hour in this layer.

Looking higher, one finds a region into which the stratosphere gradually blends where the small amount of nitrogen and oxygen remaining no longer exist in the normal 80:20 ratio, the temperature rises, drops, then rises again rapidly, and conventional airflow theory is not applicable. This region, up to about 250 miles, is known as the ionosphere because some of the molecules are broken up into ions and free electrons. A highly important feature of these ions is that they reflect radio waves; thus long-range communications are possible by "bouncing" radio signals off the ionosphere. The lower portion of the ionosphere, some 20 to 60 miles up, is sometimes identified as the chemosphere; it is here that much of the sun's energy is converted into more useful forms. Satellites have to be orbited above the chemosphere, as it is sufficiently dense to slow them up and cause them to fall back to the earth.

From 250 to 600 miles is a region called the mesosphere because it contains mesons and other cosmic particles. Beyond the mesosphere lies a region called the exosphere, meaning simply the outermost layer. Beyond is space. Actually most people who work in this field consider space as beginning at about 90 miles because satellites have to be above this level to remain in orbit. Further refinements include the terms air space (0–60 miles), aeropause (60–90 miles), near space (90–4000 miles), outer space (beyond 4000 miles), cislunar space (this side of the moon) and translunar space (beyond the moon). These terms are all defined in Appendix B.

Much is yet to be learned about the upper atmosphere and space. It is known, of course, that high temperatures, cosmic rays, and meteors are constant dangers.

As for temperature, it could rise to 4000°F inside a missile if it were not for the fact that a large part of the heat flow to a missile would be lost in radiation. A missile in space with a black skin might heat up to about 450°F; but if the surface were painted white, the temperature might be more like 100° below zero. A temperature permitting occupation by a human crew could be created by the choice of paint, if the paint could withstand ultraviolet rays.

Cosmic radiation may affect missiles adversely, because the energy of some radiation in outer space is sufficient to penetrate all parts of the weapon.

Meteors also are to be reckoned with. Their paths constantly intercepting that of the earth, they come into the atmosphere like high-speed bullets until they are vaporized by air friction at altitudes of 35 to 50 miles. The likelihood of a meteor's striking a high-altitude guided missile may not be great, but when long-duration manned spaceship flights are contemplated, meteors become an important hazard. More information on space and space travel will be found in Chapters 11 and 12.

High-Speed Flight

Guided missiles are usually designed to travel at very high speeds. This reduces the time of flight, opportunity for enemy reaction, and effectiveness of countermeasures. Any discussion of high-speed missile flight involves such terms as *sonic speed, supersonic speed, Mach number,* and *shock wave.* What do these terms mean?

Sonic speed is the speed of sound. The nature of all high-speed gas flow is dependent upon the speed of sound in that gas. Sound is a pressure variation moving through a gas, such as air, or any other medium, such as water. If the pressure variation is produced by a very small disturbance, the rate of movement of that pressure wave through the medium is predictable and constant. The speed of sound in air at sea level is about 1120 feet per second. In water it is 4720 feet per second. The speed of sound depends upon the compressibility and density of the medium. In the case of air, as we have mentioned, these two properties are altered by temperature and therefore the speed of sound changes with temperature. Actually the speed of sound is proportional to the square root of the absolute temperature. This accounts for the lower speed of sound at altitudes where the temperature is low.

Supersonic speed is greater than the speed of sound. Air flow around missiles is radically different at subsonic and supersonic speeds. Flight speeds on the order of six to ten times the speed of sound are sometimes called "hypersonic." Another term often used to describe the condition when the missile is traveling at or just above the speed of sound is "transonic." It means that, although the missile as a whole may be traveling just above the speed of

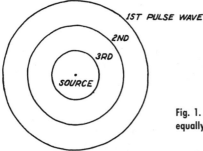

Fig. 1. A stationary source of sound sends out equally spaced spherical sound waves.

sound, local velocities along the sides of the body are sonic, sub-sonic, and supersonic. This condition may cause extreme stresses on a missile and should be passed through as quickly as possible. The crash of the British test pilot John Derry in a de Havilland 100 jet fighter demonstrated the sometimes-disastrous effects of transonic speed. In the fall of 1952, while he was flying at sonic speed, the elevators of the tail were torn off. Derry managed to land safely, but later at an air show, after a low-altitude super-sonic dive, transonic stresses ripped off the twin-boom tail and the plane disintegrated, killing the pilot instantly.

The Mach number of a flying missile is simply the ratio of the missile speed to the local speed of sound. As previously stated, the speed of sound depends upon the temperature. If the missile is at sea level and is traveling in warm air at a Mach number of 2, its speed is twice the speed of sound or about 1520 miles per hour. At an altitude of 50,000 feet where the temperature is lower, Mach 2 corresponds to a speed of about 1320 miles per hour.

A shock wave is a sudden pressure variation created by a body moving through a medium at sonic speed or higher. The shock wave can best be understood by considering a small body in air which is emitting regular sounds pulses, let us say at a rate of 1 pulse per second. If the body is standing still (Fig. 1), the sound waves move out in all directions in a spherical pattern. Each wave is separated from the previous wave by 1120 feet, the distance sounds travels in 1 second at sea level.

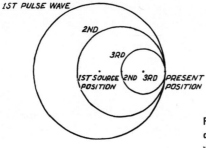

Fig. 2. The pattern of sound waves from
a source moving toward the right
with a speed equal to that of sound.

If, without changing the pulse rate, the body is made to move at the speed of sound (Fig. 2), each sound pulse will create the same spherical pattern; but the source, moving to the right, keeps up with each wave moving in that direction, causing a super-position or piling up of the sound waves just in front of the moving body. At that point the pressure variation across the multiple-strength wave is a strong one.

If the body moves faster than the speed of sound (Fig. 3), it will pass through each sound wave it creates; but the combination of all the waves produces a wave front shown by the broken lines.

The motion of a missile creates sound pulses at practically an infinite rate, and the wave front created is known as a shock wave.

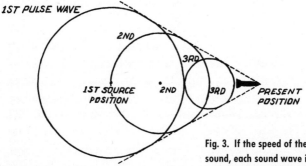

Fig. 3. If the speed of the source exceeds that of
sound, each sound wave intersects the preceding
one and they can all be enclosed in a conical
surface shown in section by the broken lines.

The word "shock" is appropriate, because there are abrupt changes in the velocity, density, pressure, and temperature of air as it flows across it. Shock waves are actually visible under certain conditions and can be photographed in wind-tunnel tests. Note also that shock waves are actually three-dimensional about a missile. The shock wave caused by the pointed nose of a supersonic projectile is conical, not merely triangular as a two-dimensional sketch would seem to indicate.

Why A Missile Flies

All forces acting on a moving missile can be resolved into four resultant forces: thrust, drag, lift, and weight (Fig. 4).

The motion of the missile depends upon the relative magnitudes

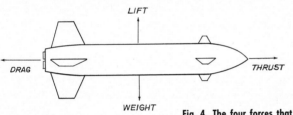

Fig. 4. The four forces that act on a moving missile.

of these forces. If the thrust of the power plant is a greater force than the drag, the missile will accelerate forward; and if the lift force is greater than the weight, the missile will rise. It is easy to understand how thrust can be produced to overcome drag, but see how lift is accomplished. If an airfoil (wing) has the proper shape and angle of attack (upward tilt of the forward edge of the airfoil), the air will flow much faster over the top of the airfoil than under the bottom. Increased velocity is always accompanied by a drop in pressure; therefore, the greater pressure beneath produces a net force upward, or lift.

Some possible airfoil cross sections are shown in Fig. 5. A subsonic airfoil does not make a good supersonic airfoil, and the reverse is also true. Note the blunt, rounded forward edge of the subsonic

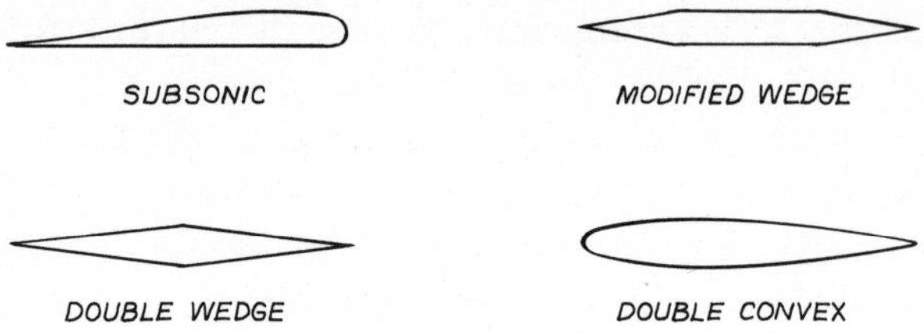

SUBSONIC

MODIFIED WEDGE

DOUBLE WEDGE

DOUBLE CONVEX

Fig. 5. Some possible airfoil cross-sections.

airfoil, so designed to produce the higher air velocity across the top surface. If this airfoil were used on a supersonic missile, the drag would be excessive.

Supersonic airfoils are characterized by sharp leading edges and are very thin. It is a considerable design problem to develop an airfoil with both thinness and sufficient strength. The modified double wedge represents a good combination of low drag and strength and is relatively easy to manufacture.

The over-all shape of airfoils may vary considerably. They may be rectangular, delta-shaped, swept back, circular, or any one of many other possibilities, depending upon their uses and the speeds involved.

To give a missile enough lift and thrust to fly is not sufficient; it must be stable as well. A missile is stable if it has the tendency to return to a position of equilibrium after it has been disturbed. The disturbance may be deliberate when the missile maneuvers, or it may be caused by forces beyond control. A missile is usually designed to be stable in pitch, yaw, and roll (see Chapter 5). That is, if the missile suddenly executes one of these motions, it has a natural tendency to correct itself. On the other hand, it is possible for a missile to be too stable, making it difficult to maneuver.

Wing surfaces, normally called the rudder, elevator, and aileron (Fig. 6), control and maneuver a guided missile. Right and left deflections of the rudder produce right and left turns of the missile. Similarly, up and down deflections of the elevators cause the missile to climb or dive. The missile flies in the new direction

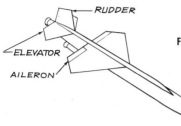

Fig. 6. The wing surfaces that control a guided missile.

because the tail has been slewed in the opposite direction, forcing the fuselage to face in a new direction. If the designer places the movable wing surfaces on the nose of the missile (called the Canard design), a left deflection produces a right turn, and so on.

The ailerons are used principally to create roll. Moving the ailerons in opposite directions creates an imbalance, which makes the missile roll. Many combinations of control surfaces are possible, but for simplicity, economy, and ease of analysis, a minimum number should be used.

The detailed aerodynamic analysis of guided missiles is an extremely complex subject requiring a good background of higher mathematics. But even theoretical studies are hard to evaluate because of the difficulty of performing satisfactory flight tests. There is no pilot in the missile to read instruments or to return the craft to base for further study. Because a flight usually ends in a crash, a missile is almost a total loss after a flight test. The missile aerodynamicist is forced to obtain technical information on the ground by radio (telemetering) and by cameras and instruments later ejected by parachute or protected to withstand the crash at the end of flight. He can also make wind-tunnel tests, but the high Mach numbers desired necessitate huge and costly structures.

Fortunately for the man who will use missiles in combat, the aerodynamic problems will be largely solved before he receives the "hardware." But this in no way lessens the vital importance of aerodynamic research and airframe design.

5. Guided and Misguided

Rocket-propelled projectiles have come to the front several times in history, but always they have been outmoded by the greater accuracy and range of guns. World War II brought free (unguided) rockets again, which were characterized by a high rate of fire, lack of recoil, and light weight of launcher. But why were they still less accurate than gunfire? Because an artillery shell has its maximum velocity and stability at the muzzle. Direction and velocity are accurately known; therefore, it is easy to predict the flight path. Jet-propelled projectiles, starting with low velocities and little stability in early flight, have poor accuracy with no guidance. With guided missiles it is the guidance that counts. A missile with malfunctioning guidance would be worthless and even dangerous to its users.

Guidance in jet-propelled missiles is essential because greater accuracy than that of conventional weapons is needed both at gun range and beyond. Also it may be necessary to alter the trajectory after launching to intercept a moving target. Unpredictable variations usually exist in the medium (air, space, or water) in which a missile moves and tend to throw it off course. Manufacturing tolerances (of weight, shape, alignment), causing no two missiles to be exactly alike, must be compensated for as well.

Let us assume that we are building a guided missile and that we want to select a guidance system for it. What are the different methods of controlling these steel-feathered firebirds? To guide a missile, we must perform two basic yet exceedingly complex tasks.

First, we must give the missile *trajectory control*. We must make it follow the most ideal path to the target. This means that we must know its position and direction of flight with respect to the target. Then deviations away from the desired trajectory can be corrected by sending signals to the missile controls to turn right or left, up or down, or to change velocity.

Second, the missile must have *attitude control*. This means that we must keep it pointing in the proper direction with the vertical fin actually vertical, and that it must know up from down. If a missile in flight has inadvertently rolled over on its right side, a signal to turn right will result in a dive.

Trajectory Control

If we consider first trajectory control, what are some of the possible ways in which we could make our missile stay on a desired path? Theoretically, it could be guided by some completely self-contained control system, by reference to the natural phenomena about it, or by the use of electromagnetic energy for some means of remote control. Some publicized examples of each of these three possibilities follow.

Self-contained internal control. Two internal control systems often mentioned are the preset and the inertial systems.

When preset guidance is used, a predetermined course is set into the missile controls before launching. This flight course takes into consideration predicted atmospheric conditions, target location, and missile performance. Once we launch the missile, it will go through the motions we set into it with complete disregard for any unexpected changes. It is on its own and we can make no corrections during flight. The German V–2 rocket, for example, had a time mechanism that caused the missile to rise vertically for the first few seconds and then pitch over into a specific angle of climb until the rocket motor was shut off. It an unpredicted tail wind caused the V–2 to move faster than expected, the huge rocket would go beyond the target.

The conventional naval torpedo is also a preset missile. It is usually set to run on a certain predetermined path. Once it has been fired, the launching crew has no more control over it.

The preset system is simple, reliable, and inexpensive, and is not vulnerable to countermeasures. But it has poor accuracy. Let's look further.

How about inertial guidance? Suppose that, when a strong tail wind gave a missile an unexpected boost in the direction of the target, a device such as the one in Fig. 7 were in the missile.

Fig. 7. An inertial accelerometer for trajectory control.

The inertia of the sliding mass would cause it to move to the rear against the coil with a force proportional to the forward acceleration of the missile. The distance the mass moves is a measure of the unwanted acceleration. This measure of acceleration can be converted almost instantly by double integration (a mathematical procedure) into the extra distance the wind is causing the missile to move. To compensate for the range error thus detected, the missile slows itself down, or dives into the target after a shorter time of flight, or cuts its motor off sooner.

We can install inertial devices such as this, called accelerometers, to measure not only the distance the missile has moved toward the target, but also its drift laterally or vertically. With this information a computer within a missile can compare the actual flight with the desired one and send corrective signals to the control surfaces. The system is completely internal and, like the preset system, it requires no outside signal and is not vulnerable to countermeasures. Theoretically it affords greater accuracy, but it is naturally more expensive, complex, and subject to malfunctions. Vibration of the missile, for example, makes instrument damping necessary; but excessive damping makes the accelerometers insensitive to high-frequency changes of direction. An ideal compromise is difficult to find.

Natural-phenomena reference. If we know the location of a target with respect to any natural phenomenon of the earth or space, and a missile can be made to use the same phenomenon for locating itself, it can be guided to the target. Some examples of this type of trajectory control are magnetic reference, altitude reference, distance reference, and celestial reference. The Germans used the first three in combination on the V–1 missile.

We can use the magnetic field of the earth by providing a compass to keep the missile on the proper heading. The dip of the magnetic needle toward the earth could also possibly be used, since the dip varies according to the location of the needle on the earth. This system is simple but not very accurate. The Germans used this system on the V–1 missile to keep it on the right heading.

The varying pressure of the atmosphere with altitude (or of water with depth) can be used to cause a missile to travel at a prescribed distance above or below sea level. A simple altimeter or pressure gauge can be connected with the control mechanism to accomplish this. The Germans used this altitude-reference system on the V–1 to fly it at 3000 to 5000 feet.

Distance reference is a method of measuring how far a missile has gone. The distance traveled toward the target can be measured by a small wind-driven (or water-driven if water-borne) propeller, which is calibrated so that a certain number of rotations represents a unit of distance traveled. The total number of rotations is counted mechanically; and when the desired distance has been traveled, the missile can be made to dive, turn, explode its warhead, or perform any other function. The V–1 was designed to go into a spiraling dive at the end of it trip.

Celestial reference is a fascinating guidance scheme we could adopt. Just as men on shipboard or plane can "shoot the stars" to determine their position, a missile could do it automatically. Star-tracking telescopes within the missile would continuously note the position of the stars. A computer could interpret this information, and appropriate signals could make the missile stay on its path to the target. When the "brain" indicated that the position of the target had been reached, the missile would automatically dive into the target. This system would naturally be complicated and expensive.

Electromagnetic control. These systems may be divided into four categories: remote control, radio navigation, energy-beam slave, and target seeking. Consider first the remote-controlled missiles. Control signals come from an outside source such as the plane, ship, or ground control station that launched the missile. One of the oldest forms of missile guidance, remote control has been used for many years in model airplanes and boats, and is now used in target planes for antiaircraft practice. Radio operators on the ground control the plane by watching it and sending signals to it to turn right or left, to climb, and so on.

One method of using remote control is to have the radio-control operator steer the missile into the target. The location of the target is known by the operator's seeing it, by his knowing its map location, or by radar's locating it. The position of the missile is known by the operator's seeing it or by having radar track it. The missile itself does not perceive the target. It merely reacts to the signals sent from the operator. In the case of supersonic missiles, such as the Nike family, the "operator" is an automatic computer; the problem is too complex and fast-moving to be solved accurately enough by a human operator.

Another method is to see the target remotely by television. A television camera and transmitter within the missile send back to the operator the picture of what the missile "sees" ahead. The operator signals the missile accordingly; and when the objective comes into sight, the missile is steered into the target. This system was employed in Korea by the United States Navy, using obsolescent aircraft as their missiles. The Air Force also did experimental work with this system during World War II. The remote-control pilot can be hundreds of miles away from the missile as long as there is line-of-sight contact between them.

A third remote-control possibility is to have the missile connected to the operator's "control box" by long, fine wire which trails out behind the weapon as it goes forward. The operator sees the target by one means or another and has direct wire contact with the missile and electrically controls it. Obviously the system is good only for short ranges, perhaps as an air-to-air or antitank missile where the operator keeps his "bird" aligned in the cross hairs of his sight, which are also on the target. The French SS–11 and other antitank missiles use this principle; the result is an extremely simple weapon.

Since in all three of the above systems an operator—human or mechanical—sends commands to the missile, these types of trajectory control are often called command control.

Radio navigation is another way to utilize electromagnetic radiation for guidance. Any navigation consists of locating oneself with respect to some system of coordinates in order to travel toward a destination that is also located in the same coordinate system. If the coordinate system is artificially generated in space by radio signals and the missile can "read" these coordinates and know the coordinates of the target, a computer within the missile can calculate the flight path to the target. For example, the radio-navigation system known as LORAN (LOng-RAnge Navigation) works this way: Two carefully located radio transmitters send out signal pulses simultaneously. These energy signals travel at the specific known speed of 186,000 miles per second. It a receiver were in a missile located exactly halfway between the two stations, the signals would arrive at the same time. Assume that the missile is launched in a direction perpendicular to a line connecting the two transmitters. If the missile deviates to the right, the signal from the right-hand station arrives first. The missile computer can measure the time delay between receipt of the signals and steer the missile back into the desired path again. If transmitter stations are located at equal distances from the target, and the missile constantly keeps itself at equal distances from the stations, it would have to fly over the target.

Another means, perhaps another pair of transmitter stations, could tell the missile when to dive into the target. This is necessary since, with only one pair of stations, the missile knows that it is on a line equidistant at all points from the stations. The intersection of this coordinate line with another produced by the second pair of stations locates the target. Actually, the target does not have to be on the equidistant line. If it is closer to one of the transmitters than the other, the time delay can be calculated and

Homing guidance all the way. The powerful target-seeking Hawk, shown here in a triple cluster, protects troops from fighter-bomber attack. (U. S. Army photograph.)

the missile can be made to fly on a line with that fixed time delay rather than no time delay. Many variations of this system are possible.

We could have our missile slaved to an energy beam. If a narrow energy beam (light, radar, infrared, or any other beam that can be made highly directional) is trained on a target, an obvious way to get to the target is to follow the beam. Thus, if a missile has internal equipment that detects its position in the beam and makes it a slave to it, an operator need only keep the beam on the target to get a hit. Even if the target is moving, the beam can follow it, and interception of the missile with the target is accomplished. The U. S. Navy Talos and Terrier air-defense missiles employ this technique.

The most intelligent missile of all, the target-seeking missile, actually perceives the target and computes its own control signals. If the missile is to "see" the target, the target must have some characteristic that distinguishes it from its background. If the target is a distinctive source of heat, light, magnetism, or radio transmission, and the missile can detect it accurately, the missile can be made to go straight for that source. (This type is known as a passive seeker.) Naturally, the enemy is not going to have the target emitting anything a missile can "home" on if he can help it. But it is possible to "illuminate" the objective by radar signals from the missile (in this case are active seeker). The U. S. Army Hawk is a target-seeking missile; so is the Navy Sidewinder.

These are some of the theoretically possible guidance systems that we could use on our missile. Many others are not mentioned, and some are probably yet to be discovered. Just which of these are practical and are actually being used is classified information. The details of their design, components, range, and accuracy, and the discussion of which types of guidance are most appropriate for certain targets must in general be avoided, too. Note that combinations of these types are possible. We could launch a missile with preset initial guidance and employ celestial navigation to the target vicinity for mid-course guidance. Finally, perhaps we could use a target-seeking system for terminal guidance.

Attitude Control

Attitude control must exist if a missile is to respond properly to guidance signals. The simplest way to control attitude is to control the angular motion of the missile in all three dimensions. These motions are known as pitch, yaw, and roll, and are shown in Fig. 8.

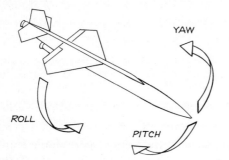

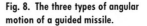

Fig. 8. The three types of angular motion of a guided missile.

For any of these motions to be detected, there must be a stable platform in the missile as a reference so that corrective signals may be sent to the control surfaces. Gyroscopes are most often used because of their ability to remain fixed in the plane of rotation of the rapidly spinning rotor (Fig. 9). The rotor is spinning in the

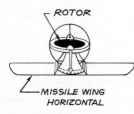

Fig. 9. A gyroscope mounted on a missile to control roll.

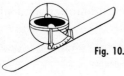

Fig. 10. When the missile rolls, the gyroscope remains fixed in space.

horizontal plane and tends to stay there. If the missile rolls as in Fig. 10, the gyroscope rotor will remain fixed. The angle of roll, measured by the angle between pointer and frame, can be detected electronically and a servomechanism actuated which causes the control surface to correct the roll error. Similarly, yaw and pitch control can be effected.

Now if in steering the missile it is necessary to roll it a few degrees for a banked turn, the pointer is turned to that angle (Fig. 11). Because the pointer is no longer aligned with the frame, an error signal is detected and the missile banks until the angle is again zero (Fig. 12).

Now if the signals generated by various guidance systems or stable platforms are amplified, they can actuate aerodynamic control surfaces and guide the missile. This assumes that moving the rudder or elevators will result in a change in motion of the missile. There are two different situations in which moving the aerodynamic control surfaces in the air stream would do no good, inasmuch as there is not enough force exerted by the air stream on the control surfaces.

The first case occurs when the missile is launched initially and does not have sufficient velocity for the air stream to act on the control surfaces. During this critical period of flight, the craft must maintain its stability some other way. A launching crew

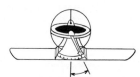

DESIRED ANGLE OF BANK

Fig. 11. A gyroscope set to produce a banked turn.

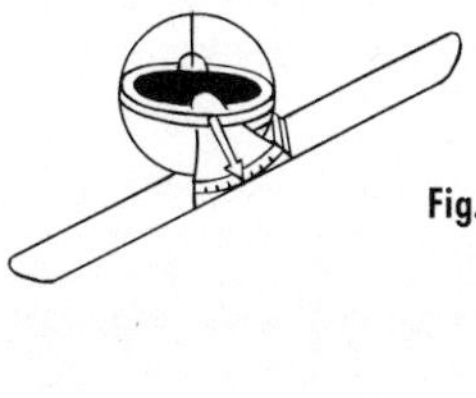

Fig. 12. A missile banks until the gyroscope setting is zero.

could place the missile within long guidance rails which restrict its motion until it is up to flying speed (just as a gun barrel restricts the shell until it is up to the necessary speed and rate of rotation), but the tactical disadvantage of a huge rail launcher is obvious.

Another scheme for overcoming low-velocity instability is to use a booster rocket to get the missile up to speed quickly. Propulsion engineers have developed boosters that have tremendous power for short time durations. These "disposable" power plants can boost even large missiles weighing several tons from launchers of no appreciable length. The Air Force Matador is launched in this manner.

Still another way to achieve low-velocity stability is to have control surfaces in the jet stream just behind the motor exhaust. The jet stream is always moving rapidly, perhaps 1 mile per second or more. Control surfaces (called jet vanes) within the jet stream, when deflected, will produce a lateral force on the tail of the missile just as normal air vanes do. Obviously, finding a material to stand the 2000° to 4000° F exhaust temperature is not easy. But the vanes need last only long enough for the missile to get up enough speed for the aerodynamic surfaces to be effective. The Germans used this technique for launching the V–2, which has jet vanes made of carbon.

Another possible answer to low-velocity stability is to mount a jet motor on gimbals so that its direction of thrust can easily be changed in response to error signals from the gyroscope.

The second situation in which normal aerodynamic control surfaces are useless exists when a missile is at very high altitudes where the atmosphere is very thin or does not exist at all. In this case gimbaled rocket motors or rocket motors exhausting in lateral directions (at right angles to the direction of flight) are necessary not only for attitude control, but for guidance as well.

A Sample Guidance Problem

For some appreciation of the problem of designing a control system, let us analyze how one might cause a missile to fly reli-

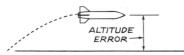

Fig. 13. A guided missile with preset altitude control has leveled out too slowly so that it is at too great an altitude.

ably and accurately at a given altitude, say at 10,000 feet. Assume that the missile will climb by preset control to 10,000 feet, where an altimeter-controlled device will automatically cause the missile to level out. By the use of a gyroscopic stable platform the missile will thereafter maintain level flight. But if at the "level-out" signal the missile happened to turn too slowly, it would end up at too high an altitude (Fig. 13). With the stable platform preventing the missile from diving or climbing, it will remain too high, and the guidance requirement is not met.

A system that will cause the missile to seek the 10,000-foot altitude is a simple "on-off" mechanism which, actuated by the altimeter, will give the elevators full up, down, or zero signal when the missile is below, above, or at 10,000 feet, respectively. As shown in Fig. 14, this system will cause the missile to over-shoot the proper altitude and continually oscillate, perhaps with increasing amplitude, until control is lost entirely. The timing of the on-off system could be advanced to anticipate the correct position of the missile, which would then remain in the vicinity of 10,000 feet; but it would still be in continual oscillation. The power requirement for operating the elevators would be high, for a full signal up or down is continuously transmitted; and because of oscillation the exact position of the missile would never be known.

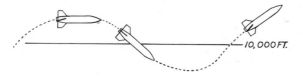

Fig. 14. A missile with a simple on-off altitude-seeking control never levels out. Note the positions of the elevator.

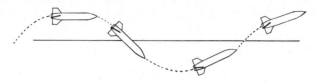

Fig. 15. Even if the elevator position is made proportional to the altitude error, the missile continues to oscillate about the desired altitude.

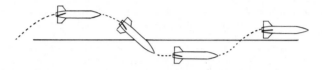

Fig. 16. If the elevator is controlled by a device that detects how fast the altitude error is changing, the altitude oscillations can be damped out so that the missile will be stable.

To decrease the power requirement we could make the elevator signal proportional to the altitude error. But this also might cause excessive oscillation. The missile could not settle down and might be divergent as well (Fig. 15). Effective damping of oscillations of the missile around 10,000 feet must be introduced somehow.

One solution is to add a device that detects how fast the altitude error is changing. If the elevator position is made proportional to the altitude error plus the rate of change of the error, so that corrective reverse elevator position is taken in time to damp out oscillations, the missile will be stable. The flight path from the initial altitude error will be as shown in Fig. 16.

A block diagram of the components of the system used in Fig. 16 is shown in Fig. 17. Note that the error signal from the altimeter is sent to two different blocks. The output voltage of the lower block is proportional to the rate of change of the error, that of the upper block to the error itself. Both signals are amplified, and the sum of the amplifier output is fed into the servo motor operating the elevator.

By referring to both Figs. 16 and 17, we can see why this system works. Initially, when the missile is in level flight at too high an altitude, a steady, unchanging voltage causes a strong down signal

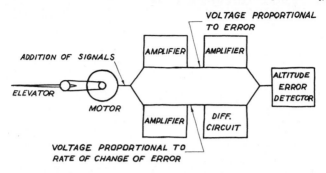

Fig. 17. A block diagram of the altitude-control system that produces the flight path shown in Fig. 16.

from the upper amplifier, but none from the lower (rate of change of position is zero). By the time the missile has reached 10,000 feet the error signal is zero, but the rate-of-change signal is a strong negative (missile-diving) signal and the elevator is in a strong up position. This prevents serious "over-shoot" of the missile and stability is accomplished.

This demonstrates how a very simple control problem might be solved. Unfortunately, the usual requirements are far more complex and necessitate complicated systems. But the principles involved have been demonstrated here.

The most revolutionary aspect of the new weapons is that they are actually *guided* missiles. The guidance is at once the most desirable feature of these craft and the most difficult to achieve. The demands for high accuracy and exacting control are often met only by accepting almost prohibitive complexity, yet the result is worth the price. But perhaps even the complexity can be lessened in time.

6. Flying Cuspidors and Stovepipes

The modern rocket motor resembles nothing so much as a nineteenth-century cuspidor. Although elongated a bit, it has the same graceful contours of chamber, narrow neck, and flared opening. Actually, an experienced fiftieth-century archaeologist digging in the ruins of our age should have no difficulty in differentiating the two. But who can say that his young assistant will not exclaim, upon unearthing a "primitive" rocket missile, "Ah, a flying cuspidor!"

Air-breathing ram jets already have the nickname of "flying stovepipes." The utter simplicity of a flying tube with a fire in the middle and an opening at each end readily lends itself to such a name. Indeed, just after World War II some scientists successfully conducted early ram-jet experiments with an exhaust pipe removed from an airplane motor.

A guided missile is usually thought of as being either ram-jet or rocket propelled, but just as there are many ways to guide a missile, also there are many ways to power it. Many propulsion systems are possible for guided missiles. The first truly guided missiles were unpowered. Launched from aircraft, they dived or glided into surface targets. Being inherently slow and having a short range, they are of limited value today.

Guided missiles could be gun-fired. Unguided projectiles of many sizes are launched by guns, but they have dispersion and inability to maneuver as their two major disadvantages. If artillery shells could be made to change course in flight, their performance could be greatly improved. The technical difficulties appear to be almost insurmountable, but the possibility should not be ignored.

Catapult propulsion could be used for launching only. The catapult gives the missile initial flying speed. Other means of propulsion have to take over for sustained flight, but the catapult is important where a short launching ramp is a requirement, as on shipboard.

Another practical possibility, because of the proved reliability of the system, is propulsion by propeller. The naval torpedo, an underwater guided missile, is propeller driven. The first attempts at flying powered remote-controlled missiles after World War I were made with propeller-driven pilotless planes. During World War II and in the Korean War obsolescent aircraft were loaded with high explosives and flown into targets by remote control. The advantage of using such conventional power is that it is readily available and efficient (at speeds less than that of sound). On the other hand, the conventional reciprocating engine and propeller combination is complicated, expensive, heavy, and too slow to be practical except in rare cases.

Of course, guided missiles can be and usually are jet propelled. The term jet propulsion includes both rockets and ducted (air-breathing) jets. The major reason for their use is that they can attain high speed. But they have other advantages, too. The jet motor is potentially a much simpler mechanism than a reciprocating engine; no warmup period is needed; no propeller torque, drag, or pitch-control problems exist. A jet power plant can withstand extreme weather variations, has light weight and a high altitude ceiling (no ceiling for a rocket), and can produce a high missile acceleration if designed for that purpose.

Not only is there a wide variety of jet power plants, but they are often used in various combinations. Rocket boosters are common for missiles that need high take-off acceleration but that use ducted jets for sustained power. Propellers and turbojets are combined into turboprop engines. But jets of one form or another are commonly used for guided missiles.

Principle of Jet Propulsion

Jet propulsion is not a new or complicated principle. It is the force that causes a toy balloon to fly about the room when inflated and released with the balloon mouth open. It is the force that causes the barrel of an artillery piece to move sharply backward (recoil) when the weapon is fired. Modern artillery recoil systems transmit the backward force so smoothly to the base on which the weapon rests that one tends to overlook the magnitude of that force. Yet, if the barrel were disconnected from the recoil system and the gun fired, the reaction would hurl the barrel many yards to the rear. The force created by the burning powder acts on both the base of the projectile and the breech of the gun. For every action there exists an equal and opposite reaction which tends to oppose the original action.

If this disconnected barrel continued to fire one projectile after another in rapid succession, as a machine gun does, the barrel would continue to recoil, gaining speed with each round. Now we have a jet-propulsion system, even if a little "rough" in operation. Such a motor was actually patented by an American in 1893. The inventor, S. B. Battey, had charges loaded and fired in machine-gun fashion, and planned to steer his rocket ship by aiming his barrel. Replace the intermittent ejection of solid bodies by constant ejection of high-velocity gases, and a workable jet motor is created. The reaction previously called recoil is now known as thrust, but it is the same reaction. Thrust is the reactive force (produced by the change of momentum of the ejected gases) exerted on the missile to propel it forward. It is usually measured in pounds and is the normal way of defining a jet motor's performance. The German V–2 motor, for example, produces a thrust of about 56,000 pounds.

It is inevitable that the question will arise, "How many horsepower is that?" The two cannot be directly compared unless the missile speed is known, since power is force times speed, whereas thrust is force alone. As a convenient approximation, 1 pound of thrust equals 1 horsepower at 375 miles per hour. Therefore, at 375 miles per hour the V–2 is developing about 56,000 horsepower. At its maximum speed of 3600 miles per hour the V–2 is developing over a half million horsepower or about the equivalent of 100 large locomotives. Install a V–2 propulsion system in the caboose of a long transcontinental freight, and the steepest grade would be no obstacle. (Actually, rocket propulsion of a railroad car was extensively experimented with in Germany.)

Another question that always comes up is, "How fast can a rocket go and what limits it to that speed?" Why did the V–2 rocket have a maximum velocity of about 5000 feet per second? Naturally air friction in the atmosphere and the force of gravity affect a missile close to the earth. But to simplify our problem let us put our missile out in space where neither gravity nor friction is significant.

Starting with Newton's basic laws, we can derive the following formula [see G. P. Sutton, *Rocket propulsion elements* (Wiley, New York, 1949), p. 236]:

$$V_m = V_g \ln\left(\frac{M_t}{M_t - M_p}\right),$$

where V_m is the maximum velocity of the missile; V_g is the velocity of the gases exhausting from the rocket motor; ln stands for the natural logarithm, the power to which e (approximately 2.718) must be raised to equal the following fraction in parentheses; M_t is the total weight of the missile at take-off; and M_p is the weight of propellant consumed.

Apply this formula to the V–2. The exhaust velocity of the V–2 was about 6000 feet per second. Its total take-off weight was about 14 tons and the weight of propellant consumed was about 9 tons. Substituting in the formula, we find $V_m = 6000 \ln 2.8$, or a little more than 6000 feet per second.

Therefore the V–2 could achieve a maximum velocity of about 6000 feet per second if it did not have to fight gravity and air friction. Notice a very significant fact revealed by this formula. In order to get high missile velocity we must either have a high exhaust velocity or a missile whose propellant weight is a high percentage of the total missile weight.

Another question frequently raised which this formula answers is, "Why not use nuclear power in rockets?" The law that as much of the total take-off weight as possible must be exhausted at the highest possible velocity sets the limit. Engineers eventually will find ways of making rocket chambers withstand the higher temperatures of higher exhaust velocities. Until they do, we shall have to depend upon the chemical fuels and oxidizers.

Another useful term in rocketry is specific impulse (symbol, I_{sp}). As a mathematical expression:

$$I_{sp} = F/W,$$

where F is the thrust and W is the amount of propellant expended per second. An indication of energy content, the unit of specific impulse is pounds of thrust per pounds of propellant consumed per second, or simply seconds. Some high-performance chemical propellants have an I_{sp} approaching 300 seconds. Liquid hydrogen and oxygen may reach 370 seconds. These values are for low altitude and are increased by 15 to 20 percent at high altitude.

In the field of jet propulsion, thrust is a far more convenient and simple measure of performance than horsepower and is used exclusively. Note again that thrust is the reaction to the exhausting of gases from the jet motor. The gases do not "push" against the air to obtain thrust. Thus, a rocket can operate with a complete absence of air; indeed, it is most efficient then.

Guided-missile jet-power plants can be divided into two basic types: ducted (air-breathing) propulsion systems and rockets.

Ducted Propulsion Systems

Consider the first type and its applications. Missiles powered by ducted jet engines carry only fuel and use atmospheric oxygen for burning. In general they have less range and fuel economy than propeller-driven craft, but vastly more than rockets. Like the phases of a conventional reciprocating-engine cycle, they have intake, compression, combustion, and exhaust. The three major variations of ducted jets are pulse jets, turbojets, and ram jets. Note the power cycle in each of these.

The pulse jet. An intermittent-firing jet, the pulse jet has a cyclic rate of 6 to 60 cycles per second. The exhaust pulsations resonating in the tailpipe of the engine produce a very loud vibration, which gives use to nicknames such as "stuttering stovepipe" or "buzz bomb." Since the pulse jet has only one moving part, the inlet-valve bank located in the intake diffuser, its primary advantage is its simplicity. The valve bank consists of a series of one-way flap valves or shutters, which periodically open and close.

To analyze this system, assume for simplicity that only two pairs of flap valves (greatly enlarged) are used instead of a multiple bank of them. Visualize the motor moving through the atmosphere fast enough to ram air into the intake diffuser (Fig. 18). This is the intake phase.

Because of the ramming action, the velocity of the air decreases and the pressure builds up until the valves open. At the same time fuel sprays into the high-pressure, low-velocity air stream (Fig. 19). This is the compression phase.

Next comes combustion. The fuel-air mixture ignites (initially by a spark plug), and the "explosion" that follows sharply raises the pressure and temperature in the combustion chamber. The combustion-chamber pressure is now much higher than the diffuser pressure, and the flap valves close (Fig. 20).

Finally comes the exhaust phase. The burning mixture under

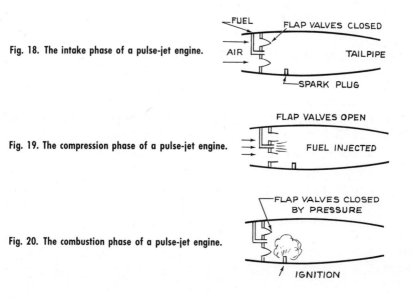

Fig. 18. The intake phase of a pulse-jet engine.

Fig. 19. The compression phase of a pulse-jet engine.

Fig. 20. The combustion phase of a pulse-jet engine.

Fig. 21. The exhaust phase of a pulse-jet engine.

high pressure violently rushes out the open tailpipe, creating the reactive thrust force that propels the missile forward (Fig. 21).

Now that the first cycle is completed, let us take another look at the intake phase to see how the cyclic rate is perpetuated. The inertia of the exhausting gases is so great that they continue to move down the tailpipe until the air pressure in the combustion chamber is lower than not only the diffuser pressure but the outside atmospheric pressure as well (Fig. 22). The flap valves will therefore automatically reopen and admit the fresh air, which is again sprayed with fuel. Also, some of the burning gases do not leave the tailpipe, but are sucked back into the combustion chamber. These hot gases and the heated walls of the engine ignite the

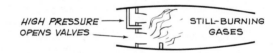

Fig. 22. The intake phase on the second cycle of a pulse-jet engine.

fresh charge, and the spark is no longer needed. Note that the motion of air into the intake duct is necessary; hence, to get the missile into motion, the launching crew usually employs a rocket booster or catapult. Once ignited, a pulse jet will produce thrust while stationary, but not enough for rapid take-off.

Being a light, simple mechanism using a cheap kerosene fuel, the pulse jet is ideally suited, from the point of view of economy, to guided-missile application. However, the compression is not good enough for efficient operation, and models thus far developed are relatively slow (maximum speed, 450 miles per hour) and have too low an altitude ceiling (10,000 feet). The German V–1 missile was the first and most famous pulse jet. Pulse-jet engines are now used for guided-missile training, for target drones, and for experimental helicopters. They will have combat-missile application in the future only if their speed can be radically increased.

The turbojet. This is the next step toward higher power and speed. It overcomes a major disadvantage of the pulse jet in that it provides an internal mechanical means of obtaining high compression instead of depending upon rapid forward motion in the atmosphere to get good intake and compression. Thus, a much wider range of speeds is possible. The schematic diagram of Fig. 23 shows how the turbojet works. Air is pulled into the ring-

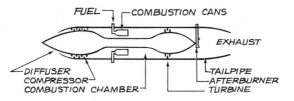

Fig. 23. The components of a turbojet engine.

shaped intake duct around the rotor of the compressor (intake). The first bank of rotating compressor blades catches the air and forces it into the next bank, and so on with ever-increasing velocity and pressure until it is exhausted into the combustion chamber (compression). As the compressed air leaves the compressor at several times atmospheric pressure, it enters a combustion chamber of constantly increasing cross-sectional area. Within the combustion chamber are perforated pipes, which consume about one-fifth of the total air mass. Fuel sprays into the air within the pipes and ignites (combustion). These pipes are known as ignition pipes or combustion cans. Hot burning gases rush from the cans, rejoin the unburned air, pass through the turbine blades, and exhaust through the tailpipe (exhaust). Note that the various phases of the power cycle occur at different positions in the turbojet simultaneously, whereas the pulse-jet operation is intermittent. This is why the turbojet has a smooth, steady delivery of power.

The action on the turbine blades produces rotation, which in turn drives the compressor. The intense heat of combustion would soon destroy the turbine blades if it were not for the fact that the large volume of air that passes around the combustion cans rejoins the combustion products. The resulting mixture is cooled to a temperature (about 1500° F or less) that the blades can stand. The combustion cans are necessary to get the ideal air-fuel ratio (about 15 : 1) for efficient high-temperature burning. The energy converted into mechanical work in the turbine is just enough to drive the compressor, yet it absorbs a considerable part of the available power.

Actually, the combustion cycle can be prolonged and the thrust increased by burning more fuel in the airstream after it leaves the turbine blades, by means of an afterburner. The purpose of this technique is to raise the temperature higher than the turbine blades could have endured. The hotter the exhaust the higher its exit velocity, and the more powerful the engine. With an afterburning turbojet engine, missiles are able to attain supersonic speed.

The schematic diagram of the turbojet shows an axial-flow compressor. A centrifugal compressor has also been developed that has some advantages, but the small frontal area and excellent performance of the axial type make it the most desirable for guided missiles.

An outstanding advantage of the turbojet is that since it mechanically provides its own compression it can be operated at a standstill. However, a large portion of the available energy is used by the compressor when the craft is stationary or moving slowly and little is left to produce thrust. Because of low power at low speeds, long runways are necessary for turbojet aircraft. As a missile (or plane) gains speed, the increased ram effect of the air into the diffuser eases the burden of the compressor and more energy is available for thrust.

The turbojet has these other advantages: it uses fuel more economically than any other jet engine; it has reached a high state of development; it is reliable; and it is available for use. It is, however, a relatively expensive and complicated power plant which is designed for long duration. Therefore, to use a turbojet on a craft that will fly only once, and perhaps only for a few minutes before it destroys itself, tends to be wasteful.

The ram jet. This is the ultimate in ducted jet engines for guided missiles, because it is capable of supersonic speeds and yet is potentially a simple and inexpensive engine. This is the "flying stovepipe." It was previously noted that the ram effect of the air in the turbojet relieved the compressor of a lot of its work at high speed. If the speed can be increased sufficiently, the compressor, and therefore the turbine, can be removed entirely, because the ramming effect alone is enough to provide the needed compression. The result is a lightweight engine with no moving parts whatever.

This is the way the ram jet works: Assume once again that the missile (Fig. 24) is moving rapidly to the left. Intake is accom-

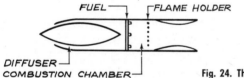

FUEL — ⌐FLAME HOLDER

DIFFUSER —
COMBUSTION CHAMBER —⌐

Fig. 24. The components of a ram-jet engine.

plished by the flow of air into the duct. Because of the large cone-shaped "island" located in the nose, air flow is momentarily restricted and slows down considerably. Actually, as the air flows around the nose toward the inlet, it passes through a series of shock waves, which raises the pressure and lowers the speed. As the air moves through the expanding diffuser section its pressure is increased and its speed decreased still more until it reaches the combustion chamber, where fuel is added and ignited. The expanded combustion gases rush out of the exhaust nozzle with vastly increased momentum (mass times velocity) compared to the momentum they had upon entering the motor. The resultant thrust forces the missile forward at high speed, well up into the supersonic region.

Two points merit special mention. First, the question of why the burning gases do not move forward out of the open nose of the missile as well as out of the exhaust needs to be answered. Principally it is because the ram-created high-pressure region forward in the diffuser section offers much higher resistance to motion in that direction than the open exhaust at merely atmospheric pressure. Also, the gases still have considerable speed rearward and their inertia makes them tend to continue to the rear. The net effect, therefore, is to expel all gases rearward.

The other point to be mentioned is related to the air velocity during combustion. Despite the slowing-down process, the air is still moving so fast that it blows out any flame placed in it unless some means is available to hold the flame there. Therefore, ram jets have a flame holder, usually a perforated metal plate, just after the fuel injectors. It provides a number of small local regions where the air velocity is so low that blowouts will not occur. The flame is initially ignited electrically, and the flame holder maintains a continuous flame throughout the combustion chamber.

Summing up, the value of the ram jet lies in its simplicity and light weight combined with enormous power output at high speed. A ram jet with thrust and velocity equivalent to a 2000-horsepower engine need weigh no more than 60 pounds. This means 0.03 pound per horsepower for a missile capable of supersonic speed. Its high altitude ceiling, perhaps eventually up to 70,000 or 80,000 feet, is another important advantage.

But for all its powerful thrust at high speed, it has none at a standstill. A booster or catapult must get a ram-jet missile up to some minimum speed before it will work at all. It is not particularly efficient until near sonic velocity. Also, a designer creates a ram jet for a particular speed and altitude combination, and it is not much good at any other. Hence, a ram jet is relatively inflexible in its use, once designed.

The ram-jet propelled Talos. Note the air intake of this air-defense missile.
(Official U. S. Navy photograph.)

Rockets

A rocket is a jet engine that, instead of using atmospheric oxygen for combustion, carries its own oxygen along. This makes the rocket-powered missile completely independent of the medium in which it operates. It is the only known power plant that is able to operate in space beyond the atmosphere. In the case of the rocket the compression phase of the power cycle is accomplished when the propellant is formed. Intake is the placing of the propellant in the combustion chamber and may be done before or during flight. Combustion and exhaust follow as in air-breathing jets.

Rockets are classified according to the type of propellant (fuel and oxidizer) used and according to their application. There are two common types of propellant: liquid and solid. Less common and thus far of little practical value are gaseous propellants and combinations of the three.

Solid-propellant rockets. A solid rocket propellant is a slow-burning explosive (containing oxygen for complete combustion) formed into a single large grain and put in the combustion chamber. When the propellant is ignited, it burns evenly on all exposed surfaces, the linear rate of burning perpendicular to the surface being dependent primarily upon the chemical content and the chamber pressure. The more propellant surface exposed, the more combustion gases are produced, the higher the pressure and thrust, and the higher the rate of burning.

If high thrust and short burning duration are desired of a given propellant, as much burning surface should be exposed as possible. A rocket motor with such a propellant is known as an unrestricted-burning motor, and is schematically shown in Fig. 25.

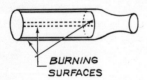

BURNING
SURFACES

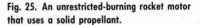

Fig. 25. An unrestricted-burning rocket motor that uses a solid propellant.

Usually the charge is so shaped that, as combustion progresses, the area of the burning surface remains constant. The chamber pressure and thrust are therefore approximately constant. In Fig. 25 the ever-decreasing outer surface area is compensated for by the increasing inner surface area of the hollow charge.

Constant thrust means not only steady and predictable performance, but reliable and safe operation as well. Radical increases in chamber pressure may cause detonation and destruction of the entire motor. Radical pressure decreases may cause the flame to go out, for most solid propellants will not burn below a specific pressure. The thrust of unrestricted propellants may be very high but the burning time is usually short.

If a longer burning time is needed, a large solid charge is fitted tightly into the combustion chamber so that only the end will be exposed to the flame (Fig. 26). When ignited, the charge will

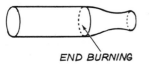

END BURNING

Fig. 26. A rocket motor in which the solid propellant burns only at the end closest to the exhaust nozzle.

burn cigarette-fashion, beginning at the end closest to the exhaust nozzle. In addition to longer burning time, restricted-burning propellants usually have lower thrust than unrestricted propellants.

The outstanding advantage of using solid-propellant rocket motors on guided missiles is simplicity. Missiles with such a propellant system are easily launched. The short-duration, high-thrust characteristics make such rocket motors ideal for boosters and for short-range guided missiles.

On the other hand, solid-propellant motors have some drawbacks that severely restrict their use. The necessary weight and size of the motor, in order to contain all of the propellant to be burned, are generally large. Solid rocket propellants do not have a long burning time. Very slow-burning grains do not have good performance characteristics even when long duration is possible. Overheating of the combustion chamber is a knotty problem, because a good cooling system is not easily adaptable to a solid-propellant motor. Also, the burning time and thrust cannot be easily varied. Once ignited, the propellant burns at full thrust until all fuel is exhausted. To control either of these variables is difficult.

Other technical problems are created by the gradual consumption of the propellant. The volume of the combustion chamber steadily increases. This tends to change the pressure and temperature, which in turn alters the thrust. Proper design shape of the propellant grain can partially compensate for this, but to get a constant thrust for a considerable period of time is not easy. Also, aerodynamic problems arise, because the missile rapidly becomes much lighter, causing changes in wing loading, the location of the center of gravity, and other factors. If solid-propellant missiles are fired in extremely hot or cold weather, their performance may be radically affected, too.

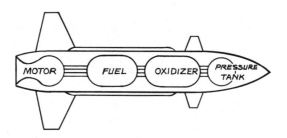

Fig. 27. The components of a liquid-propellant rocket motor.

In spite of all these problems, the military user instinctively prefers the solid propellant because of its simplicity in field use.

Liquid-propellant rockets. During the centuries when only solid propellants were available, it seemed impossible to obtain both high thrust and long duration. The answer was discovered in propellants that are fed in liquid form into the motor from storage tanks within the missile (Fig. 27). A typical liquid-propellant system would consist of a fuel tank (containing, for example, alcohol), an oxidizer tank (containing liquid oxygen), the motor, and a means to force the liquids into the motor. The propellants are sprayed into the combustion chamber, where, upon being thoroughly mixed, they are burned. The hot, high-pressure gases formed are violently expelled through the nozzle, producing the thrust.

Since the burning creates pressure within the motor, the fuel and oxidizer in the storage tanks must be under even greater pressure or else the propellants would not flow into the motor. Therefore, the missile carries along a pressure tank, as shown in Fig. 27, filled with a high-pressure gas (air or nitrogen, for example), which will force the propellants into the combustion chamber.

For larger missiles with long burning time (about ½ minute and up), this type of feed system is excessively heavy because of the necessarily large size and weight of the pressure tank. Turbine-driven pumps are often used instead to force the fuel into the motor. The turbine is usually run by chemically generated steam.

With the heat developed, the motor would soon melt if there were no cooling. The most common solution to this problem is regenerative cooling. With this system either the fuel or the oxidizer is pumped through a jacket around the motor to act as a coolant before being fed into the combustion chamber.

The liquid-propellant rocket motor can have a longer burning time than the solid, and its thrust and duration are controllable. The heat problem is more easily solved by regenerative cooling and other methods. The liquid-fuel motor gives high performance with low weight. The V–2, for example, at its maximum velocity develops 16 horsepower per pound of weight of the missile.

Weighed against these advantages is the complexity of the liquid-propellant rocket missile. Manufacture is expensive; preparation in the field is involved and time consuming. Storage and handling of fuel and oxidizers is complicated because many are dangerous or toxic or must be kept at extremely low temperature (liquid oxygen at minus 200° F).

All rockets have a high rate of propellant consumption. The V–2 burned 9 tons of alcohol and oxygen in 60 seconds. Such high propellant consumption makes the rocket unsuited for long-range level flight. However, it is the only propulsion system that is potentially capable of carrying a missile away from the earth, never to return. There is almost no limit to the size, thrust, or speed of a rocket-propelled missile. It is the newest, most modern and dramatic means of propulsion known; yet it is the oldest, dating back to Chinese antiquity.

Jet-Motor Nozzles

Perhaps one has noticed that usually the exhaust portion of a jet motor contains a narrow section which is followed by an expanding section to the end of the motor. This apparent restriction to flow is known as an exhaust nozzle, and under certain conditions it vastly improves the effectiveness of the motor.

Ordinarily when a fluid moving down a pipe comes to a narrow section, it speeds up, and then slows down again when the restriction is past. In the case of a jet motor, if the chamber pressure is sufficiently high, the speed of the combustion gases in the narrowest portion, the throat, will become equal to the speed of sound; but beyond the throat it will tend to further *increase* in velocity until, when exhausted into space, it may be several times sonic speed. Without attempting to make a technical analysis of the reason for this, we can see that this phenomenon is highly desirable, because the higher the exhaust velocity, the greater the thrust.

An equally interesting fact is that as the gases move in the diverging section from the throat to the exhaust the pressure decreases. If the exhaust is designed so that the exit pressure is equal to the atmospheric pressure about the missile, the motor is more efficient than if any pressure difference exists. Obviously, if a rocket must travel from sea level to extreme altitudes, some compromise amount of expansion must be used. Also, a rocket motor is most efficient when the flight speed equals the exhaust velocity. From these few facts it can be seen that the shape of the exhaust nozzle of a jet engine is critical and must be carefully designed.

The Quest for More Power

To obtain great range, go into an earth orbit, or escape the earth entirely, missiles must attain very high velocities. If the payloads are heavy, and they will be, the power requirements are enormous. Escape velocity is 25,000 miles per hour. With a single rocket, the velocity must be achieved either by increasing the velocity of the rocket exhaust gases or by improving the rocket's mass ratio, $M_t/(M_t - M_p)$, which is the ratio of take-off weight to empty weight when fuel is consumed. Consider these two alternatives.

From the formula on page 77, we can see that for the maximum velocity to equal the exhaust velocity, the natural logarithm of the mass ratio must be unity; that is, the mass ratio must equal the value of the base e, which is about 2.718. For a missile with this mass ratio to leave the earth, its exhaust velocity would have to be 37,000 feet per second. The highest exhaust velocity that can be obtained now with any known fuel is about 9000 feet per second, and it is unlikely that this can be increased to any startling degree.

If, on the other hand, one increases the mass ratio, the space rocket will travel faster than its own exhaust. Even if a superfuel combination such as liquid hydrogen and liquid oxygen produced a jet velocity of 12,000 feet per second, the missile would still have to obtain a final velocity of more than three times that amount. To get a missile speed three times the jet velocity, the mass ratio, 2.718, must be cubed, which means that more than 95 percent of the missile weight must be fuel. It would be a difficult, if not impossible, feat of engineering to build a missile that could hold twenty times its own empty weight in fuel. What is the would-be space traveler to do?

The effective structural weight would be reduced if we could drop off part of the tanks and engines continuously as fuel is burned and they are no longer needed. It is not possible to do this continuously, but it is possible to build the rocket in a finite number of stages, each of which, after the first, is the payload of the previous one. When the fuel in one stage burns out, the next stage separates, its engine ignites, and it leaves the heavy, useless, burned-out stage behind. A three-step chemical rocket is sufficient, if designed properly, to obtain escape velocity; but to carry a substantial payload it must be large. Von Braun's Saturn rocket will stand almost 200 feet tall on the launching pad, as high as a 20-story building. These data should at least indicate to the amateur space traveler that he cannot build his spaceship in his basement.

Even when multiple stages are used, chemical propellants have real limitations. Their use is the "brute-force" approach which somehow must be circumvented if truly significant payloads are to be lifted into space. The huge Saturn booster is the prime example of brute force in action. Its eight liquid-fueled motors combine to produce more than 1,500,000 pounds of thrust necessary to lift the total take-off weight of 500 tons or more. Solid-propellant motors of enormous dimensions are under development too. The Aerojet General Corporation has successfully fired a 100-inch-diameter solid-propellant booster containing 100 tons of propellant. The huge rocket burned for 87 seconds and developed a thrust of 500,000 pounds.

Liquid hydrogen and oxygen remain the most promising chemical approach yet unleashed. When these elements combine to form relatively light water molecules, which can be accelerated to 12,000 feet per second, a specific impulse of 370 seconds or more is theoretically possible. The trick has been to control the dangerous-423° F liquid hydrogen, which like money flashes into vaporous form at every opportunity. It appears that the Pratt and Whitney "Centaur" motor has turned the trick. The vaporizing hydrogen cools the combustion chamber, then drives a turbine which in turn pumps both the hydrogen and the oxygen, and finally burns in the combustion chamber.

However, even more sophisticated solutions are being explored. The probability of using nuclear fission is very high. One rather startling proposal is that a series of small nuclear explosions behind a protective wall would transmit impulses directly to the wall itself. A more promising approach is to use a controlled fission reactor to heat and exhaust a working fluid. A specific impulse of 1000 seconds may be possible with this method.

Objective: 1,500,000 pounds of thrust with a single engine. America's most powerful rocket engine, the F-1, will look much like this early full-scale mockup when it is ready for flight. A cluster of six engines would produce up to 9,000,000 pounds thrust and place 150,000 pounds of payload in an earth orbit. (NASA photograph.)

Another advanced solution is electrical propulsion. By the use of an electrical field, particles can be made to accelerate and exhaust at extremely high velocities. Electrical-propulsion schemes are all characterized by very low thrust and long duration, and specific impulses up to 10,000 seconds and more appear possible. Electrical propulsion is therefore most promising for application to long-distance space flights; it is of little value for take-off from the earth, because the thrust is less than the weight of the vehicle. The ion rocket is the best-known electrical-propulsion scheme. By the use of electrostatic fields, ions are accelerated and exhausted to produce thrust. Other electrical solutions include the use of an electric arc to heat and expel the propellant, and the highly theoretical photon rocket which converts energy to light and expels it.

Modern guided missiles are almost exclusively powered with jet-propulsion systems. These systems, whether of the "cuspidor" or "stovepipe" variety, have numerous advantages and disadvantages, but their big selling point is their speed potential. The rocket has the additional capability, of course, of being able to operate in space. One will see jet propulsion with increasing frequency, not only in guided missiles and other weapons of war but in peacetime applications as well.

7. Missile Payloads

The whole reason for a missile's existence is its payload. All other components provide transportation designed to put that payload at a certain place at a certain time. As missile compartments go, the payload compartment is usually the smallest of all and could contain a warhead, instruments, cargo, or even human beings. A missile can carry the large warhead of an aircraft bomb and deliver it with the speed of an artillery shell, thus combining the best features of both aircraft and gun artillery. It is costly ammunition, but the use of such a relatively expensive delivery system is justifiable considering the capability of the warhead and the accuracy with which it can be delivered.

Missiles may have any type of warhead that a bomb or artillery shell may have. Depending upon its application, the warhead may be nuclear or conventional high explosive, or it may carry some special-purpose warhead for a particular type of target. High-explosive, fragmentation, and special-purpose warheads are usually associated with highly accurate smaller missiles and are extremely effective; but the nuclear warhead is the major catalyst for missile development, especially for development of the larger missiles.

Nuclear Warheads

Missiles would have brought about a major evolution in warfare even if nuclear warheads did not exist. However, the combination of missile and nuclear warhead has revolutionized warfare; the change has been more abrupt than any other in military history. Within a few years of the first nuclear explosion, one ICBM

The Davy Crockett provides nuclear firepower for forward combat troops. The warhead was designed and developed by the Atomic Energy Commission. (U. S. Army photograph.)

can deliver a blast equivalent to many millions of tons of TNT, three men can fire a nuclear weapon, called the "Davy Crockett," capable of destroying any target on the battlefield. Warfare suddenly has two faces, utterly different, and the nuclear warhead is the reason. Why it has so much power and how it works deserves our attention.

A nuclear explosion, like a conventional chemical explosion, is caused by the release of a large amount of energy in a short time. The energy of a TNT explosion is created by a rearrangement of the hydrogen, oxygen, carbon, and nitrogen atoms that make up the TNT. On the other hand, the energy of a nuclear explosion is produced by rearrangement of the components of the atomic nuclei; hence the expression *nuclear energy*. To be a purist about this, one could correctly say that the atomic interaction of ordinary high explosives produces atomic energy, and the nuclear interaction within atoms produces nuclear energy. Thus one can accurately state that there were hundreds of thousands of atomic bombs dropped during World War II, but only two nuclear weapons.

Nuclear explosions are created either by nuclear fission or by nuclear fusion. To understand these processes, let us examine the atom itself. All elements in the universe are made up of atoms. An atom of an element is the smallest particle of that element which retains its characteristic physical and chemical properties. An atom can be broken up into its smaller components, but these have entirely different characteristics. It is by putting these components to work that a nuclear explosion is created.

An atom consists of a nucleus and a number of electrons revolving around the nucleus. The nucleus is small and dense and is made up of protons and neutrons. Protons have a positive electrical charge, but neutrons, as the name implies, are electrically neutral. These particles of a nucleus, both protons and neutrons, are known as nucleons.

Let us take hydrogen as an example. The simplest of all elements, it has only one nucleon (a proton—no neutrons present) and one electron orbiting around it. A much more complex element, natural uranium, has 238 nucleons.

With this background of information, we are now ready to see what makes the nuclear warhead release the enormous amounts of energy it does. The nuclei of all atoms consist of varying arrangements of protons and neutrons. It is a fact of nature that a proton by itself or a neutron by itself always has more mass than when that same proton or neutron is one of the constituents of an atomic nucleus. Further, the average mass per nucleon (protons and neutrons) differs for each atomic nucleus. In a nucleus of about 56 nucleons, the mass per nucleon is less than in any other combination. Figure 28 shows this phenomenon graphically.

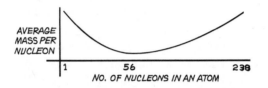

Fig. 28. The change in the average mass per nucleon with the number of nucleons in an atom. The mass is least in a nucleus of 56 nucleons.

Another fact of nature is that mass and energy are interchangeable under certain conditions. If, for example, a nucleus of uranium 235, which has 235 nucleons, is somehow fragmented into four fairly equal parts, the mass per nucleon before fragmentation is at the high right-hand end of the scale. The mass per nucleon after fragmentation is at a lower point in the scale. This "lost" mass per nucleon is converted instantaneously into energy.

The fragmenting of a heavy nucleus is accomplished by bombarding it with a neutron. With some materials, notably uranium and plutonium, in addition to the large fission fragments, several neutrons are released from the nucleus. These released neutrons collide with other nuclei in the vicinity and cause further fissions. Of course, one must realize that what appears to the eye to be solid matter is actually an array of nuclei spaced widely apart (at least 2000 nuclei diameters from each other), interspersed with many small electrons, which do not not affect the bombarding neutrons. If only a small mass of uranium is available, the neutrons created by fission can escape from the material without causing further fission. When the mass of uranium is increased until just as many neutrons escape per unit time as are created, then we have a critical amount of material and a chain reaction is barely sustained. If this amount of uranium is increased still further the neutrons build up in number and many more fissions take place in each succeeding generation of neutrons, creating a nuclear explosion.

Obviously then, for a fission weapon, the object is to keep the uranium in a safe (subcritical) configuration and, at the time the user desires an explosion, change it into a critical or supercritical configuration.

Two methods are available. The first is the projectile-and-target method (Fig. 29). Two slightly subcritical masses of uranium are

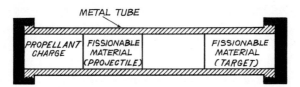

Fig. 29. The projectile-and-target method of creating a critical or supercritical configuration.

kept apart in a gun tube. The "target" mass is in a fixed position and the "projectile" mass is able to move to the right when propelled by the powder charge behind it. At the proper time, the projectile mass on the left is shot into the target mass. This must be done quickly to obtain a supercritical combination before the fissions cause it to blow apart ineffectively; therefore the gun technique is used. The gun tube also acts as a tamper to help hold the material together long enough for a great number of fissions to occur.

A second method is the implosion technique (Fig. 30). By means of explosives around the subcritical mass, the uranium is squeezed severely. This causes the nuclei to come closer together so that neutrons cannot escape as readily without colliding with

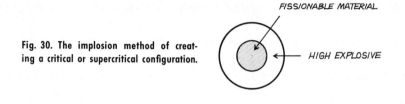

Fig. 30. The implosion method of creating a critical or supercritical configuration.

uranium nuclei. When compressed, a normally subcritical mass therefore becomes critical and a nuclear explosion results.

The fusion process is the opposite of fission: nuclei of light elements are caused to combine with one another and form heavier elements. Since extremely light elements have more mass per nucleon than the heavier elements (up to the 56-nucleon limit), mass is converted into energy and released. Fusion weapons use hydrogen or isotopes (variations) of hydrogen to be fused into a heavier element. The process requires extreme temperatures and pressures. So far the only known way to obtain the required temperature of a million or more degrees to start the fusion process is to use a fission explosion. Thus a fusion explosion is in reality a combination fission-fusion explosion.

Nuclear-Warhead Effects

When a missile's nuclear warhead explodes, it releases a large amount of energy in a very short time. Because of this great energy release, the products of the explosion and the surrounding medium are heated to temperatures of over a million degrees and turn into huge ball of white-hot gases. These gases expand with great pressure and speed, pushing away everything around the explosion until the pressure and temperature have subsided. The pressure wave created is called *blast* in air and *shock* in water or earth.

In addition to the fact that the blast effects of nuclear warheads are thousands of times more powerful than those of conventional-explosive warheads, there are two other differences. First, about a third of the nuclear energy is released in the form of heat and light. This thermal radiation causes burns and starts fires at great distances from a large nuclear explosion. Second, a nuclear explosion creates dangerous and highly penetrating rays known as nuclear radiation. In addition to the initial radiation at the time of burst, the products of the explosion remain radioactive and emit harmful radiation over an extended period of time. This long-range effect is known as *residual radioactivity*.

The energy that a nuclear explosion yields is expressed in terms of energy yields of a TNT explosion. The unit of measure is the *kiloton,* meaning the energy equivalent to that produced by the explosion of a kiloton (1000 tons) of TNT. The more powerful nuclear warheads yield energy equivalent to millions of tons of TNT exploding, hence the term *megaton* (1,000,000 tons) is also used. This unit of measure is none too large; 100-megaton weapons are already on the scene.

These are frightening amounts of energy release, with which one must deal soberly, but for comic relief we may point out that the terms *kilo* (thousand) and *mega* (million), having become quite common, have been adopted widely for amusement. Megabuck, for example, is the new convenient term for a million dollars. Think of the possibilities of the kilojigger! Most low-priced six-cylinder automobiles can go about one megafoot with a kilojigger of gasoline. If this simple figure of unity were used as the norm, it would be very easy to compare and understand gasoline consumption. Little does the average Volkswagen owner realize that he gets two megafeet to the kilojigger!

About 15 percent of the energy of a nuclear explosion takes the form of nuclear radiation. About a third of this is an initial high-energy radiation of gamma rays, similar to very powerful x-rays. Gamma rays can travel great distances and have great penetrating power. They cannot be seen or felt by human beings but they easily reach sensitive internal organs, ionize living tissue, and, in sufficient quantity, cause fatal damage to the body.

The other 10 percent of the warhead energy is released in the form of residual radiation. The fission products of a nuclear explosion are radioactive over an extended period of time, slowly decaying to more stable form. These products emit both gamma rays and beta particles. Beta particles are electrons moving at great speed. They have less penetrating power, however, and less ionizing power than gamma rays; most of them are stopped by the clothing or outer-skin layer. Beta-emitting substances are dangerous only if breathed into the body or taken in with food or drink.

A large amount of material may be made radioactive if the burst is close enough to it. A burst on or near the ground sweeps up the surface material directly beneath, irradiates it, and belches it high into the air to fall out later over a wide area. This radioactive fallout can render the area dangerous to human beings. As the radioactive material slowly drifts downward, the prevailing wind spreads it in an elongated cigar-shaped pattern over the landscape. Direct exposure to the more concentrated regions could be lethal but, fortunately for those caught in the area, there are two brighter aspects to the hazard. One is that it is fairly easy to shield oneself from the dangerous material if preparations have been made in advance. Almost any material (wood, brick, dirt, water) cuts down the penetration. The other cheerful aspect is that the radioactivity decreases with time. A lethal fallout may be safe, at least tolerable, after a few hours or at most a few days.

A nuclear-armed missile is designed to explode at a precise time in flight to achieve desired effects. These effects vary considerably depending upon whether the burst is in the atmosphere, in space, on the surface of the earth, or below the surface.

First consider the effects in the atmosphere. When the missile's triggering mechanism sets off the nuclear explosion, almost immediately a spherical ball of hot luminous gas, called the fireball, forms. In air the fireball of a 1-megaton-yield warhead may expand to more than a mile in diameter. To be classified as an air burst, this fireball must not touch the surface of the earth. The initial thermal radiation of a 1-megaton burst would be so severe that serious burns to exposed skin would occur 12 miles away and the warmth of the explosion might be felt as far as 60 miles.

The initial nuclear radiation of the 1-megaton burst would be very severe for a radius of several miles. At 2 miles about a yard of concrete, or its equivalent in other materials, would be required for radiation protection. Residual radiation would be spread over a large area but would not be likely to reach the ground soon enough to be serious unless a heavy rainfall captured the radio-active materials very shortly after the explosion and deposited them promptly on the ground.

The blast wave of the 1-megaton burst is created by the expansion of the intensely hot gases of the fireball. The front of this wave, called the shock front, is a rapidly moving wall of highly compressed air. In the first 10 seconds the shock wave moves nearly 4 miles. By the end of the first minute the wave is 12 miles away and has slowed to the speed of sound.

The strength of the blast is expressed in overpressure, which is the pressure above standard atmospheric pressure. Most structures would suffer some damage if the overpressure were 1 pound per square inch or more, although protection against higher overpressure is not too difficult. With a 1-megaton air burst this overpressure would reach out about 6 miles.

If one were to explode a nuclear warhead in space, the effects would be quite different. Perhaps the most dramatic difference is that there would be no blast wave because there is no atmosphere to transmit the wave. The pressure wave of the fireball would rapidly diminish to zero in the vacuum of space. On the other hand, the immediate radiation effects would be greatly extended. With no atmosphere to attenuate radiation effects, thermal, gamma, and beta effects would extend great distances—distances yet to be determined. Residual radiation effects would probably be negligible because the products of the explosion would be distributed over an enormous volume in a very short time. The quantity of explosion products would be small too, unless some very large target were consumed in the burst.

A surface burst is one that occurs either on the actual surface of the earth or at a height above it such that the fireball touches the surface. In either case the explosion causes both air blast and ground or water shock. The closer the burst to the surface, the more the pressure wave is absorbed as ground or water shock and the less the effects of air blast. Initial radiation effects depend upon the height of the burst point above the surface. If the burst is right at the surface of the ground or water, a great deal of the initial radiation is absorbed by the ground or water. Residual radiation is greatly increased because large quantities of dirt or water are vaporized or swept up by the explosion and contaminated with radioactivity. Even if only 5 percent of the energy of a 1-megaton-yield warhead is used to vaporize material, perhaps 20,000 tons of dirt or 100,000 tons of water are vaporized and made radioactive. The radioactive material is carried high into the air and then begins to settle gradually back to earth as contaminated particles and droplets of water. Winds spread the contamination over a large area. The powerful thermonuclear weapon detonated at Bikini Atoll in 1954 temporarily contaminated an area 250 miles long and 40 miles wide, requiring about 10 hours to spread that far.

A question sometimes raised is, "Can nuclear weapons contaminate the entire world's atmosphere and destroy all of mankind?" Neville Shute assumed the answer was affirmative in his novel *On the Beach* and painted a dismal picture of the end of the human race. The facts, however, appear to be quite the contrary. Local areas can be made lethal, but lethal contamination of the entire earth's atmosphere with nuclear weapons is virtually impossible. To attempt deliberately to end the human race, it would be necessary to detonate simultaneously thousands upon thousands of megaton warheads such as the Bikini weapon in areas equally spaced all over the earth. With sufficient density, lethal fallout could theoretically be produced everywhere, but it would rapidly degenerate into relatively harmless doses, and those who went to fallout-protection shelters would probably not be harmed.

If a nuclear warhead is burst underneath the surface of the ground or water, most of the energy appears as underground or underwater shock. Depending upon the proximity to the surface, a certain amount of the energy appears as air blast but it is greatly diminished. Much of the thermal and initial nuclear radiation is absorbed by the earth or water surrounding the burst. The result of this absorption is little initial radiation above the surface, depending on the depth at which the explosion occurs, but greatly increased residual radiation because large quantities of soil or water are contaminated.

High-Explosive and Fragmentation Warheads

Man has used explosives for centuries; long before he understood how they worked, he was surprisingly expert at rearranging combinations of atoms to cause them to release energy. Because these combinations are referred to as chemical compounds, the term *chemical explosive* is normally used to differentiate it from *nuclear explosive*. As previously mentioned, *atomic* would be a more accurate adjective for the conventional explosives that existed long before nuclear energy was discovered, but to use this term now would only create confusion.

Chemical explosives may be classified as propellants and high explosives. Propellants are explosives which burn with such low speed that they may be used to propel projectiles from gun tubes or to propel missiles, but high explosives are used in missile warheads. Their speed of burning is thousands of feet per second and, in general, the higher the burning rate the greater the brisance (shattering effect) on the surroundings. High explosives burn so rapidly the process is called a detonation.

This detonation is usually put to work in a missile warhead in one of two ways: to penetrate a heavily protected target by its blast or to propel many small projectiles grouped around the explosive. In the first case the target may be an armored vehicle or ship, or a fortification. Usually the aim is to penetrate the protection sufficiently with the blast to reach the interior or a vital part. A common way to accomplish this is to take advantage of the "shaped-charge" effect long used with explosives. This is the effect of focusing blast waves into a single very high-speed gas jet.

Assume, as shown in Fig. 31, that the missile is moving to the right and strikes the target wall. As shown, the warhead has a concave shape on the forward end. When the warhead detonates, the burning is so rapid that it reaches all parts of the ex-

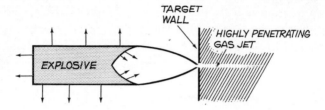

Fig. 31. A shaped-charge warhead, showing the blast wave moving perpendicularly from the surface of the explosive. It then focuses into a gas jet with sufficient pressure to penetrate to the interior of the target.

plosive before a blast wave begins to form. The blast wave then tends to move out perpendicularly from the surface of the explosive, as shown by the arrows. It can be seen that in the concave section the wave is converging on the center line. The resultant of this focused blast wave is a gas jet with speed, temperature, and pressure far greater than in any other part of the warhead blast wave.

By use of this technique, relatively small tactical missiles can penetrate many inches of the toughest steel and several feet of reinforced concrete. But they must hit the target precisely or the gas jet will not be aimed in the right direction for greatest penetration or may miss the target entirely. Hence the necessity for a highly accurate guided missile to deliver it. Antitank and anti-fortification missiles use this principle. Several nations have now equipped their armies with antitank guided missiles. Perhaps the most famous is the French SS–11, discussed in Chapter 8.

When the warhead explosive is used to propel many small projectiles, the warhead is called a fragmentation warhead. The concept is an old one. The term is derived from the artillery fragmentation shell, which on detonation fractures its own shell casing into many high-speed fragments. The old World War I shrapnel shell was a variation of this, for it was designed to eject a wide spray of pellets forward in the direction of flight. The World War II fragmentation hand grenade had its casing serrated to break up when detonated into chunks of metal of prescribed size.

Variations of these ideas are used on modern missile warheads.

BEFORE   AFTER

Fig. 32. A fragmentation warhead in which the projectile blows itself into fragments.

The object is to damage the target by striking it with projectiles that are of sufficient size and speed to be effective. The projectiles may be formed by surrounding the high explosive with a casing of rods, wire, pellets, or any other metal shapes, or even by blowing the missile itself into fragments (Fig. 32). The fragmentation warhead can be used against any target that is not well protected, but aircraft are particularly vulnerable. Of course, the warhead must be detonated within lethal range of the aircraft; the missile's guidance system sees to that. The detonation may be initiated by a fuze sensitive to the shock of impact, by an electronic proximity fuze that senses the target's presence, or by a signal from outside the missile.

Instrument Payloads

Missiles are normally thought of as having combat missions, as being warhead-carrying rockets bound for target and self-destruction. Indeed, this is their primary role, but another role has developed as well—that of carrying an instrument payload. The first instrument payloads were meters designed to measure temperatures, rate of fuel consumption, actions of components, and other such features within the missile, and to telegraph the information back to the missile's operaters. This practice led to the expression *telemetering*, which has come to represent a field of technology in itself. Instrument payloads have been designed to measure not only conditions within the missile, but the environment without. They are now being designed to perform various services as orbiting satellites. These applications are discussed in Chapter 11.

Personnel and Cargo Payloads

On May 5, 1961, a Redstone missile rose confidently off its launcher at Cape Canaveral, Florida, and pointed its nose toward the fringes of space. Gradually gathering speed, it lifted its payload high above the atmosphere and then coasted silently and and weightlessly through the void of space. The cone-shaped payload section separated from the booster shortly after the fuel was exhausted. Reversing its attitude so that the heat shield on the base of the cone was forward, it plunged earthward until the drag of the upper atmosphere began to slow it down. Then a small parachute opened and retarded it still more. Finally, a large chute opened and set the cone down easily in the Atlantic Ocean, 300 miles from the launching pad. A helicopter fished the payload out of the water, a human payload named Alan Shepard. Although the thrill of a lifetime for Commander Shepard, this ballistic-trajectory ride was only a forerunner of the main event, John Glenn's manned orbital flight the following February 20.

Fantastic, yes, but human missile payloads are now a reality. Far from being a mere stunt, this NASA-directed venture, a phase of Project Mercury, was a practical demonstration of the feasibility of human passenger delivery by missile. As shown in Fig. 33, the passenger rides with his back against the base of the cone-shaped spacecraft so that acceleration of the missile in ascent forces him against the padded back contoured to his physique. On descent, the cone enters the atmosphere base first and the 8 to 10 "g" deceleration from air friction again presses him against his contoured seat back.

Other features have been added to insure survival of the passenger and to improve his performance and comfort. The environmental-control system creates an artificial atmosphere. The system releases oxygen to maintain a pressure of 5 pounds per square inch (sea-level pressure is 14.7 pounds per square inch). The carbon dioxide exhaled by the passenger is removed by chemicals, and additional devices absorb water vapor and other gases. The temperature of the oxygen-rich artificial atmosphere is kept down to a comfortable level by a unique cooling system, boiling water off into space.

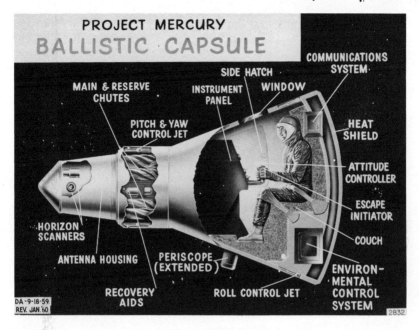

Fig. 33. Cut-away view of the Project Mercury ballistic capsule.

The passenger also has a window and a periscope from which he can view the earth and the stars. He has an instrument panel, communication with earth stations, and a number of devices to assure his safe return to earth. These devices include a heat shield to protect the astronaut from the enormous heat generated on re-entry into the earth's atmosphere, two parachutes for the final stage of flight, and a number of aids to assure that he will be found, once back on earth.

The obvious application of this knowledge will come with the exploration of space. Missile boosters will be replaced by huge rocket-powered vehicles designed specifically for passenger travel, and relatively simple missile nose cones will be replaced by large spacecraft. In addition to delivery of man into space, missiles may be used to deliver passengers quickly from one point on earth to another. Intercontinental travel of only 30 minutes duration is possible, though a bit expensive for commercial purposes. The cost

Manned missile or missiled man? A new twin-jet rocket-propulsion system developed by Bell Aerosystem Company being demonstrated at Fort Eustis, Virginia. Here a test engineer "leaps" over a truck with ease. (U. S. Army photograph.)

of intercontinental rocket passenger delivery? About $1,000,000 (one megabuck, in beatnik) per ticket today; perhaps only a few thousand dollars by 1965 or 1970. Commercial aviation too was expensive at one time. A well-known American scientist said of flying machines in 1907: "For passenger traffic the number carried will be so small and the cost so great that no competition is possible with existing modes of transit."

Even if the expense does raise budgeteers' eyebrows, the military value of rocket delivery of troops may justify further development. Visualize the impact of several companies of infantry arriving at any critical point on earth within half an hour of their departure time. Such troops could accomplish special missions or hold a critical airfield, bridge, or other key objective until additional forces arrived.

A manned payload could also perform military tasks in flight. The joint Air Force–NASA project Dyna-Soar (dynamic soaring) is exploring this possibility. The Dyna-Soar craft will be rocket-boosted into a suborbital flight path somewhat similar to the Mercury-Redstone flight except that its range will be much greater, even enough to circumnavigate the earth. Upon reentry into the atmosphere, the pilot will be able to maneuver and glide his craft to a controlled landing.

Be it nuclear explosive, high explosive, chemicals, instruments, cargo, or human beings, the content of the relatively tiny compartment in the forward tip of the missile is the whole reason for its existence. Fascinating adventure lies ahead for the human race if the right payloads are used; the tragedy of war if the lethal ones are used.

8. Missiles and Control of Land Areas

Wars are fought for the control of land and the people occupying it. Naval, strategic-missile, or space superiority are but intermediate steps toward the ultimate objective. There is no question, of course, of the value of superiority in the intermediate areas—particularly for the United States, which must defend a continent and support overseas allies. Yet one must keep in proper perspective the vital role of the forces that control the land.

The more productive the land a nation controls, the more military power of all forms it can sustain. The land provides the minerals and fuels to produce and operate weapons, and the industrial power, the manpower, and the food needed to prosecute a war. With additional land comes maneuver room to add depth and dispersion to defense. These are the reasons an aggressive nation seeks to expand its boundaries and develop buffer states. The advent of nuclear missiles does not change the importance of controlling the land and its people.

Never again will there be a major war without the use or potential use of nuclear weapons. Their threat will overshadow any battle, whether or not they are used. There is no choice but to be ready for the use of both nuclear and nonnuclear weapons in land operations; for the new god of war is two-faced.

The Land Battle of the Future

Because of the continuing threat of open warfare, much attention has been directed recently to what a war might be like, particularly if it is a nuclear war. Recent history certainly provides some clues. When one considers the impact of technology and the nature of the Communist threat, two lessons of the actions in Korea, Indochina, the Suez, Hungary, Lebanon, and the Congo are inescapable. One is the decisiveness of rapidly committed ground forces. The converse was also shown; for when sufficient ground forces were not rapidly deployed to a critical area, the results were failure. The other lesson is the validity of maintaining a strong strategic nuclear-delivery capability. Without it we would have found the Communists acting far more boldly in the recent crises.

With these lessons in mind let us imagine what the battle for control of the land might be like. Such visualization is not easy, and the problems that loom before us are enormous. The urgent need for new operational concepts, mobility, and firepower to cope with the two-faced threat has posed, and continues to pose, a genuine challenge for military planners. An army must be able to operate in jungles, temperate-zone plains, deserts, mountains, and extreme cold. It must also be able to cope with, and assist its allies to cope with, subversion and guerrilla warfare. Now superimpose a nuclear environment on all of these variables.

The problems are especially difficult because no one has had any experience with nuclear weapons on the battlefield. No one wants the experience, for that matter; but the point is that without it the discussion of nuclear tactics is largely conjecture. We can, however, visualize without too much difficulty the salient characteristics of warfare in an environment of nuclear missiles.

The land battle will be characterized by the imminent threat of nuclear weapons, whether they are used or not. This constant threat will force alteration of almost everything military forces do in war.

When nuclear missiles are used, the battle will probably consist of extended nonnuclear periods of feints, minor clashes, and even major attacks followed by short violent nuclear onslaughts. Nuclear-tipped missiles will bring sudden heavy casualties to the units they hit, even completely destroy them, unless they are fully prepared. Sudden high losses in turn will create great fluctuations in evacuation and medical support needs and in replacement requirements.

Combat units adequately armed with tactical nuclear fire-power, and able to use it freely, will find themselves able to attack and defeat much larger enemy units, especially those whose nuclear weapons or doctrine for employment give them less flexibility. A corollary to this thesis is that, in defense, no unit will be able to hold any given piece of ground indefinitely by occupation alone.

Nuclear warfare will also be characterized by devastation in rear areas equal to or greater than that along the line of contact with the enemy. A commander can use large weapons against his opponents' rear without endangering his own forces, and he has the opportunity to defeat his adversary by destroying his lines of supply. Extensive nuclear-missile attacks deep in the enemy's rear will seriously cripple a supply system dependent upon large permanent or semipermanent supply installations and surface transportation routes.

Nuclear attacks will produce obstacles to surface movement everywhere. Bridges, defiles, and transportation centers will be rendered unusable. Debris and radiation will hinder cross-country movement; air movement and supply will often be mandatory.

The land battle will also be characterized by highly effective air defense. Modern air-defense missiles will radically reduce the chances of aircraft survival over defended enemy territory. Only by the use of earth-hugging air vehicles and by counterattack of air-defense systems will large-scale air movement be possible.

Battles and preludes to battles will also feature intensive surveillance efforts, by highly sophisticated means, to locate the enemy. Countersurveillance measures will be equally intensive, for units will soon learn that to be fixed in location is tantamount to being destroyed.

These are revolutionary changes in battlefield environment that demand revolutionary changes in methods of operation; minor alterations in tactics, equipment, or organization will not suffice. As a parallel, call to mind the final play of a football game. The offensive team, trailing by six points, lines up with ends wide for a desperation pass. In this situation the defensive team does more than edge its ends out another foot. The defense spreads out as widely and deeply as possible, dispersing to counter the inevitable pass. It is a radical departure from conventional defense necessitated by a radical means of attack.

The introduction of nuclear means of attack on the battlefield is even more radical, comparatively speaking, than the introduction of the desperation pass on the football field. In the offensive, small, highly mobile combat teams must be able to move from dispersed positions (where they do not present worthwhile targets) with great speed and stealth to the focal point of the attack. They must strike rapidly and, once the mission is accomplished, quickly disperse again to avoid a counterblow. The defense must present to the attacking enemy small, tough, and elusive combat teams that refuse to hold any particular piece of ground sacred, yet force the attacker to pay dearly for all ground he takes. The defensive teams must be so concealed, protected, and dispersed that the over-all framework of defense can absorb nuclear attacks without shattering.

Combat teams, on the offense or defense, must be conditioned to accept, as normal, combat in any direction. They must be able to employ small nuclear weapons and they must be able to call for and get, with minimum delay, nonnuclear and nuclear fires ranging from conventional high-explosive shells to megaton blasts delivered by missile artillery far to the rear.

These same combat teams must be effective in a nonnuclear environment as well. Even in nuclear war there will be many situations when nuclear weapons will not be used. Beyond this, there will be major campaigns, indeed entire wars, fought without the launching of a single nuclear-armed missile. Has it not already been so in the years we have been able to split the atom? So the combat teams, like the members of a football team, must be able to close in tight for the conventional attack or defense or disperse for the radical.

In addition to these new operational concepts, consider the revolution in mobility that is needed. Before mechanization, the speed of armies was about 2½ miles an hour and the greatest distance that average units could move on foot, without rest, and still be able to accomplish a combat mission upon reaching their destination was about 25 miles. By use of the most modern armored personnel carriers and tanks, we can perhaps multiply by four both the speed and range of cross-country movement before stopping for refueling and maintenance of vehicles.

How much effort will it take to increase mobility still further? It will take a very great effort, yet we must increase our mobility to survive. To be fixed is to be destroyed. There will be times when we should be able to move at least 100 miles per hour for 1,000 miles. This means air mechanization; ground mechanization is not enough. An air-mechanized unit's ability to strike anywhere along a front and penetrate deeply into the enemy's vitals would force the enemy to dissipate its strength over wide areas and improve the attacker's opportunities to defeat him in detail. Obviously, the most promising army combat transport is the airplane.

It is extremely interesting to note the effect of the introduction of guided missiles on the airplane. Because missiles are assuming many of the combat missions of aircraft, aircraft as weapons systems are decreasing in importance. On the other hand, because missiles and other technological developments force armies to become hypermobile, the airplane as a means of transport is gradually increasing in importance. As a note of caution, however, it is not intended to imply that in another war each individual will have his own airplane—but he had better be able to get into an airplane with his weapons. Otherwise he may never even reach the scene of the battle before it is over.

With the development of such hypermobility, many targets once considered strategic because of their distance behind enemy lines have become tactical. Indeed, the concept of dividing strategic and tactical employment by measure of distance is probably obsolete. If troops or materiel that can be moved into battle within a few hours are tactical targets, then is not an enemy division enplaning a thousand miles away for a combat mission a tactical target?

Tactical objectives are also getting deeper and deeper into

enemy territory. Not only are enemy airfields, supply centers, strategic reserves, and other targets moving deeper into hostile territory, but also one's own troops may be making deep penetrations. A modern army will not be forced to accomplish an important mission at a location hundreds of miles away by painfully fighting overland to the objective. Troops will move by ground-hugging aircraft to that objective. They should be preceded by missile-artillery attacks to disrupt the defense, by air-mechanized patrols to seize air-landing areas, and by air-mechanized cavalry to suppress air-defense weapons and block counterattacks on the route of movement.

It should not be construed that air movement will be the only means of transport, or that one should be concerned only with improving strategic mobility. The demand for greater ground mobility should be met as well. Greatly improved carriers of all types capable of high cross-country mobility must be developed. These range from small command vehicles to "overland trains" for logistic support. Strategic sealift is no less important: fast naval vessels designed for tactical loading and unloading of complete units are needed also. Nor does air movement necessarily mean parachute operations. As ground forces become air mechanized, the need for parachute units will decrease.

That is the revolution in operational concepts and mobility. The revolution in firepower is the introduction of a family of weapons ranging from new, highly efficient small arms to long-range guided-missile artillery.

What types of missiles should be an integral part of United States ground forces? They are surface-to-surface, air- and missile-defense, surveillance, and transport missiles.

Included in the first group are two types of SSM's. The first is a family of relatively short-range assault weapons with high accuracy and penetrating power. The second is a series of ballistic artillery missiles that will supplement and extend the range of gun artillery.

The second category, air- and missile-defense missiles, is needed to defend army forces from attack. At least three different missiles are required. One is necessary to counter the ground-hugging aircraft performing in their many roles. A second should seek out and destroy supersonic aircraft from the hilltops to medium altitude—perhaps 40,000 feet. A third is necessary to counter incoming ballistic missiles and—should the enemy still attempt to use them—high altitude manned bombers.

The surveillance missile is needed for obtaining vital battle-area intelligence. The extent of the battle area, the need for rapid and accurate collection of tactical intelligence, and the high risk of loss of manned aircraft to hostile air-defense weapons necessitate the development of this missile.

A family of transport missiles may be required to deliver high-priority personnel and cargo from several thousand yards to several thousand miles. This means of transport combines the features of high speed, low vulnerability, and (one would hope) soft landing.

Now let us study each of these classes of missiles in more detail.

Surface-To-Surface Missiles

The range of SSM's in the land battle will vary tremendously. At one extreme is the small missile with a range of only a few hundred yards; at the other is the large ballistic-trajectory rocket carrying a nuclear warhead hundreds of miles into enemy territory.

Despite the disparity of range and other aspects of these missiles, they should have several characteristics in common. Perhaps the most important is rugged simplicity. An SSM found on the battlefield will not be a sleek, sophisticated electronic wizard serviced in air-conditioned ready rooms and supported by elaborate and permanently installed computers and radars. It must be a weapon that can still be fired after a long cross-country move, rainstorms striking, the missile transport lurching into a muddy ditch, and the fire-control officer and half the missile crewmen becoming casualties. A popular magazine once disparagingly referred to a new missile as being "blunt and unsophisticated." Paradoxically, these are much-sought-after characteristics. The SSM's that participate in the land battle had better be "blunt and unsophisticated."

Surface-to-surface missiles should have a minimum of guidance (consistent with the accuracy requirement) for simplicity and immunity to countermeasures, and should use solid-propellant rocket motors. There should be a minimum number of types of missiles and they should have a maximum similarity in design, operation, and maintenance. Each type of missile should have a clear superiority to gun artillery before being adopted, and each, insofar as possible, should have a dual nuclear and nonnuclear capability.

Let us consider in turn assault weapons and the classic categories of light, medium, heavy, and very heavy field artillery, and determine to what extent missiles will take over their roles.

Assault weapons. In recent wars assault weapons have been used for direct fire on prepared positions and fortifications in support of infantry assault, and for defense against tanks. In form, they have included many varieties of towed and self-propelled mounts. Special-purpose weapons have been developed that can meet to a limited extent either the offensive or the defensive requirement, but not a single satisfactory weapon exists that can be superior at both antitank defense and assault fire against a prepared enemy. The closest thing to it is the tank which, oddly enough, should not be used for either mission if it can be avoided.

The desirable characteristics of tanks are their battlefield mobility, armor-protected firepower, and shock effect. They should be employed to exploit a breakthrough, not to create it, and they are used to best advantage in the fast-moving offensive, not in passive antitank defense. It is true that, because the tank is still the best defense against enemy armor, a commander threatened with an armored attack must tie his own tanks down to a defensive antitank role. A frequent suggestion is that an inexpensive tank-destroyer vehicle firing guided missiles could free the tank of its defensive role. Another theory is that the tank is inadequate in its primary role anyway, because its great weight and size limit both its air transportability and its mobility for cross-country operations. One recommended replacement is a much smaller tank armed with guided missiles. Is this a reasonable proposal?

Three distinct combat roles are being combined in such a proposal: antitank defense, assault fire against prepared positions, and combat exploitation.

Ideally, an antitank weapon should be able to destroy tanks without itself being destroyed. The greatest weakness of the present weapon, the gun, is that its attrition rate is about the same as that of the target. An antitank system needs superior range, accuracy, armor protection, agility, and concealment of position. The antitank gun falls short of the ideal in several respects. Whether towed or carried on a tank, it is heavy, quickly worn out by its high-velocity shells, and cannot easily hit a moving target. Its protection, agility, range, and accuracy are, at best, the same as those of its intended target.

The missile does offer promise of improvement. A missile scarcely larger than heavy antitank-gun ammunition could be designed to deliver a warhead capable of destroying any tank in existence. It could be fired from a vehicle, a simple ground mount, or an aircraft. Several nations are now developing such weapons. An example is the French SS–11. This powerful little tank killer is only about 4 feet long and weighs only about 62 pounds. It is guided by command signals sent from the controller to the missile through fine wires laid by the missile itself. It can be man-handled or carried on any type of vehicle. Its effective range is much greater than that of an antitank gun and its warhead is reportedly able to penetrate 20 inches of steel plate.

By the use of command guidance, antitank crews could fire an antitank missile from behind a hill or any spot remote from the controller, thus making it extremely difficult for the target tank to counter. A rocket-propelled missile, producing no shock or recoil and requiring no heavy gun tube or supporting mechanism, can be mounted on light vehicles and even aircraft.

Antitank missiles have shortcomings too. They are more expensive and complex than gun ammunition and, because of their cost, training is expensive. If visual observation of the target and missile is required, the weapon is ineffective in darkness, heavy fog, or smoke. There will probably always be some minimum effective range, that is, an initial distance the missile must go from launch to attain sufficient speed, stability, and control before it can be guided into the target. For the near future this may be several hundred yards. A target closer than this minimum could not be engaged.

Aircraft-launched antitank missiles represent a significant advance in coping with the armored threat; indeed, they may become the scourge of tanks. Despite their seeming vulnerability, helicopters and other terrain-hugging aircraft can converge on a tank column from dispersed positions, execute surprise attacks from the flanks and rear, and retire with a speed and agility many times that of the tanks. Perhaps the biggest advantage of the airborne antitank weapon is this mobility. As long as the missiles remain relatively expensive and require specially trained personnel, they will be in short supply. Since antitank coverage over large areas will be required, one way to cover the areas with a limited number of missiles is to mount them on air vehicles. They can be centrally located and come to threatened points on call.

To defend themselves against such a threat, tanks or vehicles accompanying tanks will be obliged to carry antiaircraft weapons, probably missiles, designed for just such aerial targets. Thus the classic seesaw of offense versus defense will continue.

Missiles also offer considerable opportunity for improvement in assault fire against prepared defensive positions. Consider the weapons now available. In the attack of prepared positions and fortifications, the tank is the only adequately armored vehicle with a gun that has direct-fire accuracy and penetrating power. But it falls short of the desired goal because its firepower is not sufficient for destruction of heavy reinforced-concrete pillboxes and heavy embankments of earth, stone, and logs. Direct fire with large-caliber field artillery also is often inadequate, even when it can get close enough. Aircraft bombs and unguided rockets have the power, but not the accuracy, to hit such small and usually camouflaged targets. There is need for a highly accurate, penetrating, and preferably recoilless weapon for assault fire. It is doubtful that the small missile just proposed for antitank defense would have enough punch except for attack of light and temporary

Scourge of tanks. The HU-1A "Iroquois" fires the SS-11 antitank guided
rocket during a firepower demonstration. (U. S. Army photograph.)

fortifications. Of course, against the smaller targets—of which there will be many in mobile combat—it will serve admirably; but it needs a big brother to play siege gun.

In the exploitation role, the tank is in its proper element. The enemy's main defense has been breached, and his vital but poorly defended rear area is exposed. The targets the tank will meet in exploitation are personnel, unprotected vehicles and supplies, hastily constructed defenses, and antitank weapons including tanks. Is today's tank properly designed for this role? A vehicle with high mobility, range, and a versatile weapon to attack the varied targets is needed. The modern tank does not have these attributes in proper proportion; it cannot, for above all else it must be able to defeat enemy tanks. Therefore it mounts a heavy, special-purpose, high-velocity gun, and wraps about itself all the armor it can possibly carry. The product is not a weapon of exploitation but of defense.

The light assault missile previously suggested for antitank defense and for light fortifications may be the answer to the problem. If the missile could be made small enough, it would permit the use of a lighter vehicle carrying a good missile supply. A variety of warheads, plus infantry weapons, might give it the versatility desired; but the missiles will be expensive, require a more highly trained crew, and may always have a minimum effective range some other weapon must cover.

There is a natural reluctance to remove the high-velocity gun and protective armor from the exploitation vehicle. The gun is reliable, accurate, and effective; the armor protects the crew from many weapons. The new U. S. Army M60 tank, for example, mounts a powerful British-manufactured 105-millimeter gun and has retained both armor protection and impressive range (400 miles) by the use of diesel power and aluminum as well as steel. This tank is the finest that modern technology can produce. It is desperately needed in quantity and will not soon become obsolete.

As antitank missiles and air mechanization develop further, however, the heavy gun-carrying tank in future years may become less and less able to accomplish its exploitation role. It will have neither sufficient range nor mobility to make the rapid thrusts required and will not be able to cope with the antitank defenses encountered. The day may well come when columns of such vehicles, if exposed in exploitation, would be turned into rows of blazing 50-ton crematoriums before they ever reached the objective.

Probably, in time, two distinct combat vehicles will emerge and both will be missile armed. One will be an exploitation-and-reconnaissance weapon with the classic missions of cavalry. It will carry light assault missiles as its primary weapon, and infantry with small arms to add versatility. It will have great range and mobility; eventually it may be airborne. Air mechanization is the future trend and this vehicle may be no exception.

The other combat vehicle will be a tough defensive slugger designed to absorb punishment, even close nuclear bursts. It will have a short-range offensive capability but its strategic role will be defensive. It will be used to hold the crucial areas seized by more mobile, but vulnerable, forces.

Neither of these will provide an adequate assault weapon for permanent fortifications. Admittedly the massive types of forts of the two world wars will probably never again have to be assaulted, but targets too tough for a light assault missile will have to be reduced. A medium assault missile will have to be used.

Field-artillery weapons. It has been emphasized that the trend in the land battle is in the direction of mobility and dispersion. With the threat of nuclear weapons imposed on the battle scene, combat units will tend to operate in widely separated independent units and to by-pass enemy strong points if targets beyond are more important. In more stable situations, combat units may tend to hug the enemy's lines to cause him to hesitate to use nuclear weapons lest he destroy his own forces. Large areas behind these forward units may be virtually empty. The classic belt of artillery battalions, 3000 to 6000 yards deep and as long as the front, lying just behind the bayonets, may no longer be present. It is too vulnerable an area in nuclear war.

This places the artilleryman on the horns of a dilemma. His

mission is to provide fire support for mobile forces that expect to penetrate deep into hostile territory, by-passing fragmented but battle-able enemy troops as they move on. If the artilleryman follows behind these mobile forces in an area not actually cleared of the enemy, he is in acute danger of being attacked and over-run. If he adopts the slogan of the battle-wise infantryman of World War II and decides that "safety lies forward"—in the closest possible proximity to the combat arms he is supporting—he must have the same mobility they have. But the size and complexity of most of his weapons preclude this. The only alternative some artillerymen see is to give their weapons additional range so that they can site them in friendly territory at greater distances from the troops they are supporting.

To resolve the dilemma, the artilleryman must accept both alternatives. He must both join the forward elements and provide fire support from ever-greater distances. Even if these distances are hundreds of miles, the basic field-artillery problems remain. In past wars the infantryman was supported by heavy artillery that could not always go anywhere he could. In the attack he would jump off from an area just in front of the big guns and move forward to his objective. He would seize the objective and hold it, or accomplish whatever other mission was required of him. The entire action, requiring from several hours to several days, might be supported by artillery that never changed its firing position but that could deliver firepower over a wide area.

The fact that the artillery may be sited hundreds of miles from the maneuver forces does not alter the basic concept; it remains a tactical situation. However, it does alter the weapons. A modern army in the field needs an artillery arm capable of delivering fire over a wide spectrum of range and warhead effects. To borrow the artilleryman's terminology and method of classification, here is what a family of light, medium, heavy, and very heavy artillery should be like (Since artillery ranges are always expressed in meters, the terms are used here with the reminder that a meter is only slightly more (1.1) than a yard.)

The light artillery must be able to accompany the combat team wherever it goes and provide both nuclear and nonnuclear firepower. Ideally, one weapon should be used, but this may not be technically feasible. The conventional fragmentation shells should be delivered by cannon artillery (mortars and howitzers of 100- to 120-mm bore and 500 to 15,000 meters in range). In close support, gun tubes provide a rate, quality, and precision of fire support that missiles cannot emulate. They also have the mobility and logistic simplicity that is needed. As for nuclear shells, if the same gun tubes cannot fire them, then another weapon will have to be present. If the decision is ever made to "go nuclear," the combat team must have its own small nuclear weapons. The U. S. Army's first-generation weapon for this role is the famous Davy Crockett.

Medium artillery should consist of a medium howitzer (150 to 175-mm bore and 3000- to 20,000-meter range) and a medium assault missile. One or the other of these weapons could have a nuclear capability, but their value on a nuclear battlefield may be rather limited. Both have very important nonnuclear roles. The howitzer adds power and range to the light artillery, and the medium assault missile, mentioned earlier, is the antifortification weapon and should be similar in design and operation to the light assault missile to simplify logistics and training.

Heavy artillery should include one or two unguided (or minimum-guidance) rockets to cover a range spectrum of 5000 to 50,000 meters (about 3 to 31 miles). They should have both nuclear and nonnuclear warheads. The "Honest John" rocket is an example of this type of artillery. A rugged and simple weapon, the Honest John is fired from a short rail mounted on a truck. It is aimed and fired just like gun artillery and, after its 100,000-pound-thrust rocket motor burns 4½ seconds, it follows a ballistic trajectory like an artillery shell. Heavy artillery currently includes gun artillery as well. There is a good possibility that, even if heavy missile artillery becomes more accurate than gun artillery, the latter will be retained for its economy and logistic simplicity, especially in nonnuclear warfare.

Very heavy artillery should reach from 50 kilometers to about 1500 kilometers (31 to 930 miles). Probably at least two missiles

"Old Reliable." The Honest John commands the respect of friend and foe alike. It is shown here being transferred from rocket trailer to launcher. (U. S. Army photograph.)

will cover this range spread; they should be highly mobile, guided, solid-propellant, nuclear-armed missiles capable of quick reaction when fire is needed. A 1500-kilometer missile will reach almost all targets that could directly affect the land battle; its range will be commensurate with the deep air-mechanized thrusts that will come in modern war. This category of artillery includes what is commonly known today as short- and medium-range ballistic missiles. The U. S. Army Sergeant and Pershing are examples, although the Pershing, in its present form does not have adequate range. It is a second-generation system intended to replace the Redstone missile. The Pershing is smaller, lighter, more mobile, and simpler to employ than the Redstone. With inertial guidance

An NCO with a mighty punch. The Sergeant missile on its erecter-launcher. (U. S. Army photograph.)

and two-stage, solid-propellant rocket power, the Pershing is accurate and reliable. Its mobile transporter-launcher can move into an unprepared position and fire within minutes. The missile system is helicopter transportable, making it easy to carry anywhere.

Consider how these weapons might be tactically employed. The light and medium artillery provide the close support. At ranges beyond about 15 miles, the targets will be major troop concentrations, supply dumps, and vehicle concentrations. Missiles will also attack targets deep in enemy territory for the purpose of isolating the battle area. In Western Europe, for example, the Rhine bridges were prime isolation targets during World War II. The first truly tactical employment of missile artillery was an isolation-bombardment mission against a Rhine bridge at Remagen. The Germans fired about a dozen V–2 rockets at the bridge, but the accuracy was so poor that most of the U. S. troops in the vicinity did not even know that they were being attacked. Had the V–2 had the accuracy and warhead of today's missiles, the results would have been entirely different. Missiles will also attack many deep targets for destruction of the target itself rather than to disrupt the enemy transportation or communication system.

In offensive operations, an army can employ missile artillery to support any maneuver. In a penetration, it can support the main effort directly and also conduct isolation bombardment of the area to prevent the enemy from committing his reserves against the penetrating force. In an envelopment, isolation bombardment will immobilize the enemy being engaged and hinder the movement of his reserves to the critical flank. The attack of any bottleneck developing in the enemy rear area as a result of the completed envelopment may also be decisive. In a pursuit operation or in a turning movement, the long range can be used to great advantage. In fact, missiles will be particularly useful in any operation where the rate or nature of movement makes gun-artillery support inadequate. For example, in amphibious, airborne, jungle, and mountain operations, missiles can supplement close fire-support weapons from great distances.

Tactical missiles must be mobile. The Pershing missile and its self-propelled launcher. (U. S. Army photograph.)

In the defense, missiles will play a most vital role. If the enemy is on the offensive, he must abandon his protective positions and concentrate his forces for the attack. Just as he attacks, he is highly vulnerable; and the defending artillery units do not have to move long distances to meet an attack at an unexpected point. The range of the weapons will permit the rapid shift of fire to any point along an extremely wide front.

The defensive potentialities of missiles are awesome. It is doubtful that any preponderance of enemy forces will be able to eliminate defensive fire by mobile missile systems until the launching sites are physically overrun. The continuous employment by the Germans of the V–2 to the very last, in spite of overwhelming opposition in the air and on the ground, proved this principle. Only the inferior performance characteristics of the V–weapons prevented their widespread use in this defensive role. Hannibal's tricking the enemy into attacking to his own disadvantage was made a classic at Cannae in 216 B.C.; with SSM's in the hands of a bold defender, the Cannae maneuver is as modern as nuclear energy itself.

In Chapter 2 it was suggested that a great danger in warfare is adherence to a dogmatic solution, and that there will always be a well-known dogmatic solution to every military situation—neat, plausible, and wrong. Is there a dogmatic solution to the use of artillery power—missile artillery, nuclear armed? There is indeed; it is the habitual relegating of this power to a supporting role. Artillery has always been so used, the concept is time tested, and the technique is feasible. Yet to adhere to this concept, once nuclear weapons have appeared, would not only dissipate combat power, it could invite disaster.

The mission of a military force is to destory the enemy. Before the scientist brought nuclear firepower to the battlefield, it was sound doctrine to close with and destroy the enemy by maneuver. Artillery played a supporting role; the maneuvering force had the primary mission.

Today this relationship has abruptly changed. Nuclear artillery can totally destroy enemy forces within the effective radii of its bursts. It will often be the dominant means of attack, with maneuver secondary. There will even be circumstances when no maneuver will be required. For example, there may be times when an unsupported nuclear attack can destroy the enemy in a defensive position, demolish his supplies, or deny him the use of critical areas.

It is certainly possible to visualize nuclear fire supporting a main attack by assaulting troops, but such a situation may turn out to be the exception. Nuclear artillery power may, and should most frequently, make the main attack. Troop assault or other maneuver should support. There will, of course, be times when nuclear missiles will support a maneuver or be used without support. But as long as the words "Nuclear Fire-Support Plan" appear as normal terminology in operation orders or military field manuals, there is the gravest danger that the weapons which will dominate the battlefield will be habitually placed in a subordinate role. No military doctrine could be more obsolete or dangerous than the doctrine that nuclear firepower is simply additional supporting firepower.

Air- And Missile-Defense Missiles

The air and missile defense of a large unit in the field will be a highly integrated, centrally controlled system, semiautomatic in operation. Targets will be rapidly assigned and reassigned to air/missile-defense batteries as they attempt to penetrate the defended area.

The long-range and medium-range SAM's needed by an army in battle can be the same weapons used in defense of strategic targets in the homeland except that their firing units will be more mobile. An outstanding example of these weapons is the U. S. Army Nike-Hercules. A sleek, supersonic, nuclear-armed guided rocket, it can cope with any operational combat aircraft and many missiles existing today, and represents only the second generation of what is yet to come.

Because piloted aircraft will have an increasingly difficult time surviving at higher altitudes, they may rely more on very low-level attacks. At treetop height they can escape detection longer as they approach the target, take better advantage of surprise, and better avoid being shot down. A forward-battle-area air defense will counter low-flying planes somewhat differently from an air defense of rear-area strategic targets. It was stated in Chapter 2 that there is a minimum range within which fixed-trajectory air-defense weapons (guns and unguided rockets) may be superior to guided missiles. This is especially true of the field army in combat, because enemy aircraft can approach their targets low over their own territory, thus giving the defenders minimum warning time. The defense finds itself suddenly engaged at close range. But the defense will eventually meet even this type of attack with SAM's. U. S. Army weapons such as the "Hawk," "Mauler," and "Redeye" are aimed at this intruder.

Surveillance Missiles

Battle-area surveillance is vital not only for the employment of missiles, but also for the conduct of all aspects of combat operations. Combat units must discover and accurately locate forward-area targets and targets deep in enemy territory. After attacks, intelligence specialists must make damage analyses of targets. The commander must determine the capabilities of enemy forces many miles away. Superior combat intelligence is a prerequisite to success in modern battle.

One of the important requirements for achieving superior combat intelligence is that a reliable means of collection exist. Consider this requirement for a moment. Obviously visual, photographic, and radar reconnaissance must be utilized to the fullest extent. These means are all used with piloted reconnaissance aircraft, but eventually the reconnaissance plane will have great difficulty surviving over enemy ground forces. Thus the battle-area surveillance missile will be introduced. It will be a fast, returnable, and reusable atmospheric jet craft utilizing many advanced scientific techniques such as high-speed photography, infrared, and radar to gather military information.

The Red-Eye gives air defense to the doughboy. This tiny target-seeking missile will answer sudden close-in air attacks. (U. S. Army photograph.)

Whatever means is used, a field army needs rapid, frequent, and accurate surveillance deep into enemy-held territory. In time, the surveillance guided missile will prove to be the superior means.

Transport Missiles

Throughout the development history of the various missiles and their applications, as each new possibility dawned in men's minds, it was at once labeled by some as fantastic—an absurd, proposal. Other more conservative ideas, mainly improvements of existing products, might be acceptable, yes, but not this! This is going too far! Such rigid, ponderous attitudes were evidenced by responsible and informed persons occupying key positions when the V–2 rocket was conceived, when the SAM, ASM, IRBM, ICBM, and anti-ICBM were conceived.

We are now at this stage with respect to the transport missile. It is just too fantastic, too expensive, too complicated and unreliable, and too impractical, its opponents say, as earlier opponents in earlier days said about missiles in other roles.

In the enthusiasts' corner: Both tactically and strategically, there has always been a need to transport troops and supplies to critical points in a battle or campaign in the shortest possible time. As the means of accomplishment improve, so do the countermeasures to prevent their use. The most recent and dramatic means is the airplane; however, because of improvements in air-defense weapons, the vulnerability of air movement over a defended area has so increased that air transport is now too costly in lives and materiel. Therefore, ballistic rocket transports should be used as special-purpose vehicles in those situations where their characteristics are particularly valuable.

One situation certain to occur frequently in future warfare is that of supplying the isolated combat unit. The fluid-warfare concept practically guarantees that every combat unit will be cut off from its source of supply from time to time. A few centuries ago this problem did not particularly disturb the Duke of Marlborough in his famous Rhine campaign. He merely gave everyone a five-day supply of biscuits and ammunition and abandoned his source of supply five days at a time. Fortunately, he always managed to reattach himself to a base of supply before he used up what he carried. The modern combat commander likewise may often be obliged to move away from his source of supply, and the intervening area may be enemy occupied just when his supplies run low. What should he do if air resupply is attempted, but planes, pilots, and precious payloads are all sacrificed to murderous enemy air-defense weapons? A ballistic cargo missile is required to deliver the now desperately needed supplies.

The opponents logically point out that we already have too many special-purpose devices; it is a logistic nightmare to keep them available and maintain them. They claim that the situation just described must be kept the exception and not permitted to be the rule. Being the exception, we cannot afford it; for we cannot budget for every exception.

Unfortunately, it may not be the exception. The nuclear potential, the guerrilla threat, and air mobility dictate otherwise. There are several techniques that will keep the cost down. We can utilize modifications of missiles already available, and control their use at a high level to insure that they are employed only when necessary. Another possibility is a cheap, reusable propulsion section that can be recovered and reloaded (ideally with a universal fuel that propels howitzer shells, rocket weapons, and vehicles alike). Perhaps, if this proves possible, the same propulsion section can be used for delivery of warheads and cargo payloads.

With respect to strategic transport missiles, the enthusiasts become even more enthusiastic and the opponents even more vociferous.

Consider first the necessity for strategic mobility, particularly intercontinental mobility. Whether as a follow-up of nuclear attacks in general war or as main attacks in limited wars, we must move sizable forces as rapidly as possible across oceans and continents. They must be able to engage in combat upon arrival, and they must arrive soon enough to be effective. The forces to be moved include troops armed with relatively lightweight weapons and air-transportable vehicles. There will also be mechanized forces whose heavy materiel (tanks and self-propelled artillery) makes sea transport a necessity. All combat forces, even including mechanized forces, could conceivably be air transported, and strategic aircraft capable of delivering the heaviest army loads should be developed. But the quantity to be transported, whatever the weight of individual items, necessitates that sea transport be available as well.

Because of the missile threat against airfields and ports, air and sea transports must have the ability to unload without the use of such facilities. The latter should, of course, be used wherever possible because they are efficient and usually accessible to storage areas and overland routes of communications. Therefore, wherever possible, airfields and ports must be seized immediately. If these are denied to our forces by enemy occupation or by destruction, or because there are no suitable facilities in the area (as is frequently the case), air transports must be able to make water landings on rivers, lakes, or bays and unload there. This means water-based transport aircraft. Sea transports must be able to unload across beaches, and this means roll-on roll-off sea transports plus floating wharves.

But even these second-choice areas have to be seized and held in order for seaplanes or ships to unload. The employment of defensive missiles must be suppressed first by seizure of air-landing areas and neutralization of local air defense *before* the air transports arrive. Then the air-transported troops must enlarge the seized area to the coast and allow for reinforcement by sea.

Some faster and less vulnerable means than air or sea transport is needed for the opening phases of an overseas combat action where troops are not already stationed. The day will come when there will be urgent need for an extremely rapid and relatively invulnerable means of delivering advance echelons of combat troops, perhaps up to a battle group, and critical supplies from one continent to another. Travel time of an hour or less should be the goal. The time element and the vulnerability of all other means dictates that the transport vehicle be a ballistic missile with a built-in "soft" landing. The strategic missile transport may also be needed for delivery of special-forces troops and supplies deep into hostile territory. Combat forces will use it to precede major air- and sea-transported assaults, and seize ports and other vital installations to assure entry of the main body of troops.

The missile could be used in the cold war to make a show of force or come to the aid of another country in a sudden emergency. Visualize the impact of a dozen or more huge-payload capsules floating to earth by parachute, further slowed by retro-rockets, and disgorging fifty or more combat-ready soldiers each. Once set up in advance, this scene could be reproduced in an hour or two anywhere on earth from launching points within the United States and with a rocket booster under development today. This booster is the Saturn, a missile which could, for example, deliver 25 tons of useful payload from Cape Canaveral, Florida, to anywhere in Africa in thirty minutes.

Impact on the Land Battle

Modern armies must be prepared for the nuclear battlefield. The holocaust may never come, or it may come in some limited form, but ground forces must be ready to fight in such an environment.

In the event of the ultimate tragic absurdity, total nuclear war between two large countries such as Russia and the United States, there is no guarantee that the issue would be decided strictly by an interchange of ballistic missiles. No matter how vast the devastation on both sides, the decision would be reached when one side seized and controlled the other's land or made its intent and ability to invade so obvious and imminent that capitulation would be inevitable.

How should an army be organized for this decisive battle? For the strategic offensive we should use small, helicopter-transportable combat teams of battalion or even company size organized, along with supporting units, into air-mechanized divisions. These teams should be hypermobile, striking enemy forces from the rear, from the flanks, and from the air. They should be able to make rapid penetrations to accomplish specific missions and not be designed for sustained combat. They should rely on speed and firepower, and should be equipped with the best possible air transportation, weapons (especially nuclear), and communications.

Supporting these striking forces should be armored forces to provide sustained combat capability. They should be used in a strategic defensive, a flexible "Siegfried Line." Tactically the armor would be an offensive weapon, but strategically it would be used to hold areas seized by the air-transported battle groups. It should be used in defense in conjunction with natural and man-made barriers so that the strategic effect would be the same as the former use of fortifications. The defensive force must be a mobile armored force in nuclear warfare; permanent fortifications will be vaporized.

Armor is best used in strategic defense. It is admirably suited to survive nuclear attacks because of its armor protection and tactical mobility, and it is superb for limited-objective counteroffensives to throw back an enemy penetration. It is, of course, a powerful offensive force, but only in a tactical sense, for armored units have limited strategic mobility. Their strategic movements will be slow in an age of air and missile transport. Logistic limitations will not normally permit their use in the rapid and deep penetrations that will be required. Road and bridge construction requirements alone may prohibit their use in this role except in special cases. Construction in a nuclear war may not be able to compete with destruction in the conduct of decisive overland operations, especially when bridges, heavy forests, and buildings are blown down to block natural routes of attack and supply, and vital terrain bottlenecks are contaminated with radioactivity. A deep armored strategic penetration would be heavily dependent upon extensive, time-consuming, forward-area construction, creating intolerable resistance to the strategic mobility that the army must have. Armored units have a staggering fuel-resupply problem as well. Therefore they should be used to close up behind the air-transported assaults, hold the ground, and protect the missile units and logistic installations behind them.

This means two types of divisions, air mechanized and armored. For nuclear warfare both should consist of an appropriate number of battalions and three to five intermediate headquarters to control them. Logistic support should come direct to the battalions. Insofar as possible, artillery should accompany the battalions and a minimum should be employed at division level. Most missile artillery should be corps artillery. When in the nonnuclear role, however, such divisions would be woefully short of cannon artillery and would have to be greatly augmented.

The air-mechanized divisions are airborne only in the sense that air-lifted vehicles are used. The vehicles will often be ground hugging and will use protected avenues of approach. Parachutes will not be used; the vehicles will seldom get high enough. The penetration routes will be cleared by nuclear-armed reconnaissance units, also airborne—and perhaps some day for special missions, missile borne.

Divisions of such an army, if strategically prelocated, could appear almost anywhere in the world within twenty-four hours. They could be immediately available to our allies. If we look far enough into the future, perhaps their missile-transported advance echelons could arrive in an hour or so from time of request. The main body could begin to arrive by air a half-day after that, and sea transport could follow up.

In addition to the divisions, many other forces would be involved. Missile commands already stationed in foreign lands could provide nuclear firepower to allied forces not possessing nuclear weapons. These commands, which exist today, are unusual because they are artillery-heavy combined-arms teams rather than the usual choices of infantry or armor-heavy teams. The 4th Missile Command in Korea, for example, deployed there to support the Republic of Korea Army, could be moved quickly by air to any part of the Far East.

Other nondivisional forces would be additional artillery, air-mechanized cavalry, air-support and air-defense, and logistic-support units. All these forces must be capable of engaging in general nuclear war or in any form of limited war, whether the limitation is on choice of weapons or on extent of the battle area.

There is every reason to believe that a future war between great nations will still have to include a struggle for control of the land, and that the strategic missile attack, though horrendous, will have to be followed with a manpower assault. It is quite likely that the strategic missile attack, while always a threat, will invite such retaliation in kind that it may never occur at all.

Should nuclear war come, the military leader must be able to evaluate in proper perspective the whole gamut of battlefield technology. And he had better watch out, in his preoccupation with supersonic nuclear missiles, that some half-clothed, hungry, and ill-trained enemy infantryman doesn't destroy him with a subsonic, unguided, nonnuclear bayonet.

In short, a modern military force must be capable of fighting either a nuclear or nonnuclear war, for the new god of war is two-faced. Whether or not the weapons used are nuclear, their use must be accompanied by the ability to follow with physical occupation. Otherwise war will be either indecisive or will be made decisive only by senseless and total destruction, and the defeat of the very aim we seek—lasting peace.

Army forces capable of seizing objectives must be used to force the enemy to maneuver into vulnerable situations. To do this, they must have firepower integrated into their maneuver. Their commander must control both the maneuvering elements and the fire-support elements, no matter how distant one is from the other. If he does not, the metronome of firepower application will always be several beats behind the need, and chaos will result.

The application of this firepower must be either from within small, highly mobile battle groups or from launching sites far to the rear. The vulnerability of the large missile units and the nature of their logistics dictate the greater range.

Two principles remain unchanged, whatever the outcome of technological developments. The soldier must occupy the ground to insure victory, and his leader must have flexibility of mind to meet the ever-changing battle scene. If these two principles are observed, a combat force is likely to succeed in future battles. If they are not observed, it cannot succeed.

9. Control of the Seas

To counter the insidious threat of Communism, the United States must be able to control vital sea areas. In an all-out general war with no holds barred, a limited war such as Korea, or a cold war of insurgency such as exists now in Southeast Asia, control of the seas is mandatory.

In general war, a major component of our strategic missile counterattack should be the submarine-launched ballistic missile. The advantages of this weapon system and its role in strategic missile attack and defense are discussed in Chapter 10. Certainly some degree of control of the sea is needed to assure the launching submarine's freedom of maneuver and attack. Control of the sea in general war is also vital because eventually the nuclear attack must be followed by physical occupation of the enemy homeland. Significant numbers of troops can be moved and supplied only by ocean transport; for this reason also, we must control the sea.

Control of the sea is particularly important to strategic missile defense. Should the enemy ever launch a nuclear attack, it will surely include submarine-launched ballistic missiles. This is such a serious threat, and so difficult to counter, that it constitutes perhaps the number one naval problem—denial of waters, especially adjacent to our coasts, to missile-launching submarines.

The enemy, too, would be obliged to follow his nuclear assault with invasion and, if the oceans are the only routes of approach, our control of these oceans can make victory impossible for him.

In limited war, we must be able to move rapidly to any part of the world with ground forces, seize land, and establish military control over that land until such control can be restored to proper political authority. The transportation problem again makes control of the sea mandatory.

In the cold war in which we are now engaged, our ability to use freely the world's oceans is no less important. Newly emerging nations, often plagued with Communist insurgency and psychological warfare, have the will and natural ability to build themselves up, but to grow they need food and materials as well as technical advice. Sea routes provide the bulk of these, for great tonnages are involved. Interference with our use of the sea lanes in this effort would be intolerable.

As long as the antagonists are on different continents, there will be no aspect of either nuclear or limited warfare that will not be affected by control of the seas. This is a classic concept which the revolution in warfare has not changed; what has changed is the strategic role of naval forces.

The Strategic Role of Naval Forces

Long-range submarine-launched, ballistic missiles enable forces at sea to attack distant inland targets with minimum risk to themselves. This single fact has revolutionized the strategic role of naval forces.

The great American naval strategist, Admiral Alfred T. Mahan (1840–1914), with remarkable vision in his own time, described sea power as fundamentally the control of sea communications. He also wrote, "Naval strategy has for its end to found, support, and increase, as well in peace as in war, the sea power of a country." For many decades there was no alteration in this fundamental concept. Even in recent years some writers have placed total emphasis on the control of sea transportation. One may read, "All naval enterprise—with the exception of bombardment of land objectives from the sea, which is only an incidental use of sea power—is directed toward the single aim of affecting the movements of the lowly freighter or transport . . ."

Technology has forced this philosophy into obsolescence, for it has thrust an additional strategic mission upon ships at sea. Not only do missiles extend the range of a ship's striking power, but the ship extends the range of missiles even more. Nuclear-powered ballistic-missile submarines have an almost unlimited range, potentially higher speeds than surface ships, and the ability to engage directly in strategic missile warfare. This is not control of the seas; this is nuclear deterrence. It is not sea power either; it is strategic missile power.

Sea power, like air or land power, is an obsolete term. It is no longer subject to accurate definition in warfare. Perhaps the only purely naval battles of the future will consist of undersea warfare between submarines. The label of sea power should not be given to transport power and strategic missile power. If two modern, self-sufficient, warring nations are widely separated, by land or sea areas, ultimate victory will probably come to the one with superior transport power. If that area of separation be ocean, then for the foreseeable future, superiority of ocean and air transport will be vital. Control of the seas is, of course, fundamental to this superiority.

But naval forces are no longer limited to the maintenance of transport power. It has been proposed in the past that "navies exist chiefly to aid and sustain armies and air forces, and it is the latter which achieve the final decision." In the light of modern military developments, naval forces can be seen to have an additional and revolutionary strategic mission: direct attack of an enemy heartland.

The purpose of this chapter, however, is to analyze the impact of modern missile technology on military control of the seas. The first step in this analysis is to take a look at the "tools of the trade," modern combat vessels and their armament.

Modern Combat Vessels and Their Missiles

The "family" of new U. S. Navy ships of the 1960's would hardly be recognizable to the sailor of the 1940's, for the revolution in warfare has extended to ship design as well. Some of the names have been retained, but missions, tactics, and weapons have been drastically altered—altered by the advent of missiles and nuclear energy. Ship-to-ship and ship-to-shore gunnery is a thing of the past, and so are the battleships and cruisers that engaged in it. Aircraft carriers have new configurations, missions, and aircraft. New cruisers, destroyers, and destroyer-escorts now have highly specialized missions. A new category of surface ship, the frigate, has been introduced. Submarines have undergone the greatest changes of all.

Carriers. Modern aircraft carriers appear in three forms: attack carriers (U. S. Navy designation, CVA), support carriers (CVS), and amphibious assault ships (LPH).

The most modern attack carriers are of two basic sizes. One is the *Forrestal*-class carrier displacing about 60,000 tons. Its deck is about 1,000 feet long and 250 feet wide. The other is the new nuclear-powered *Enterprise*. It displaces about 85,000 tons, is over 1100 feet long, and is the only ship of its class. Both types are characterized particularly by their two landing decks, one behind the other and canted to the left, but the nuclear-powered *Enterprise* represents a significant improvement over the *Forrestal* class. Despite its similarity to the *Forrestal* in appearance, it is an entirely different ship. It is powered by eight nuclear reactors that can drive its steam turbines for five years without refueling. Thus it can travel at high speed for long periods without concern for fuel conservation. Since no exhaust funnels or boiler air intakes are used, the superstructure design and battle-damage control is improved, and radioactive or biological agents are more easily nullified.

The nuclear-powered giant is designed to carry four Terrier air-defense missile batteries, one mounted at each quadrant of the huge flight deck. An interesting aspect of this ship, however, is that it may never carry air-defense missiles or guns, but will depend entirely upon its aircraft and accompanying ships for air defense.

The flight deck is serviced from below by four aircraft elevators. The *Enterprise* can carry twice as much aircraft fuel as the *Forrestal*. Powerful new catapults for take-off, strengthened decks, and new arresting gear permit the operations of the most modern supersonic aircraft.

Carriers serve as mobile airfields wherever the employment of aircraft is desired. High-performance, jet-powered combat aircraft are placing greater and greater demands on their carriers and on the pilots who must operate from the carriers. In the past fifteen years, the speed of aircraft has increased from half the speed of sound to more than twice the speed of sound. Landing and take-off speeds have nearly tripled. Hence the requirement for the huge 60,000-and 85,000-ton carriers. Modern high-performance aircraft simply cannot operate from the old World War II carriers. Also, modern missile-armed aircraft require greatly increased storage space for fuel and ammunition.

Attack carrier-based aircraft are equipped with both air-to-surface and air-to-air missiles. The "Bullpup" is an outstanding example of an offensive ASM. This highly accurate and reliable missile has sufficient range to permit the launching aircraft to attack without closing in on the target. It is used for attacking both ships and land targets. The Bullpup is remotely controlled by the pilot, using radio command control. He watches the missile visually and guides it into the target. The "Sidewinder" and the "Sparrow III" are the air-to-air missiles currently with the fleet. The former is a short-range infrared-homing missile which has actually been proven in combat by the Chinese Nationalist Air Force against Communist attackers. The Sparrow III is a longer-range, all-weather, radar-homing missile capable of being fired at any angle of attack.

At least two carriers are assigned to a fleet to insure adequate air cover for the fleet and for any amphibious action taking place. This then is the role of the carrier with its squadrons of planes aboard: to protect the fleet and to make offensive strikes either in support of land combat operations, on sea targets to insure control of the seas, or on inland strategic targets.

Support carriers are modified World War II carriers designed to support other forces at sea with anti-submarine protection. The support carrier is usually employed as the nucleus of the antisubmarine warfare hunter-killer group. It carries the latest anti-submarine equipment including sonar, special antisubmarine aircraft, and helicopters.

Amphibious assault ships are used to launch helicopter-borne troop assaults on enemy shores. They are 20-knot ships displacing 18,000 tons, designed to carry 2000 troops, 30 helicopters, and 900 tons of helicopter-transportable supplies. These ships are not users of missiles but are, rather, by-products of missile developments. Nuclear-armed missiles make mass amphibious assaults—of the World War II variety—with their concentration of shipping close to shore, slow movement to shore, and crowded beaches, far too risky. Helicopter-borne assaults can cross any beach, avoid coastal defenses, and remain sufficiently dispersed to minimize counter-measures. It will be well to watch this radically new form of carrier. Its mission has a permanence that will not soon render it obsolete.

Cruisers. These vessels are combat ships displacing from 5000 to 30,000 tons and varying in length from about 500 to 800 feet. They are usually much bigger than 5000 tons, but a recently launched French guided-missile cruiser, called a "pocket cruiser," displaces only 5000 tons. It is armed with both air-defense and antisubmarine missiles.

The new U. S. Navy cruisers (designated variously as CAG's, CG's, and CLG's) all have one feature in common: they are guided-missile ships and their primary role is that of air defense. One, the *Long Beach*, is nuclear powered and others have varying combinations of weapons, but all are designed and used for defending the fleet at sea against air attack. The only cruiser not employed in this manner is the command ship, the USS *Northampton*. Gun batteries on cruisers are being replaced by missiles such as the "Talos," "Terrier," and "Tartar."

The Talos is the primary air-defense armament. This highly sophisticated ram-jet missile can reach out more than 65 miles and destroy attacking aircraft. Often found on board the cruiser as secondary air-defense armament is the intermediate-range, solid-propellant rocket known as Terrier. This rocket is about 15 feet

Specialization is the modern trend. The guided-missile cruiser "Canberra," whose specialty is air defense, still retains offensive firepower as a secondary capability. (Official U. S. Navy photograph.)

long and weighs about 3000 pounds. The Tartar, also used as secondary armament, is a "short"-range, solid-propellant, rocket-powered missile. Characterized by its high rate of fire and relatively close-in defense, it can nevertheless reach targets above 50,000 feet and over ten miles away.

The antisubmarine weapons carried by modern cruisers will include "Weapon Alfa," a homing torpedo, and the "Asroc." Weapon Alfa is a 12¾-inch diameter rocket that projects a depth charge several hundred yards from the launching ship. The torpedo is a medium-range, underwater, acoustically guided missile

Shipboard storage and preparation. Technicians prepare a Talos guided missile for its launcher aboard the guided-missile cruiser USS "Galveston." (Official U. S. Navy photograph.)

that automatically seeks its target. Asroc is a long-range missile that first moves through the air, then dives into the water and attacks the target.

Frigates. The next ship in descending order of size, is the guided-missile frigate (DLG). Displacing about 5300 tons, it too, has a primarily defensive role. Its size, speed, and endurance are built in to enable it to operate with carrier task forces under the most adverse weather conditions. It is armed with Terriers, Asrocs, and a few guns. Tartars will eventually appear on some. Frigates are conventionally powered, for the most part, but nuclear power is highly desirable for this type of ship too. The USS *Bainbridge* is the first example of a nuclear-powered guided-missile frigate.

Destroyers. Modern destroyers (DD), slim and fast, may be more than 400 feet long, but displace less then 5000 tons. The latest modernization programs are converting destroyers too into guided-missile ships. The Tartar, designed for the destroyer, will be installed for air defense; some dual-purpose guns will be retained, however. New submarine-detection equipment, an antisubmarine rocket launcher (Asroc), two torpedo launchers, and two drone antisubmarine helicopters will be featured. The drone (unmanned) helicopters are able to carry torpedoes and thus attack targets at great range.

Destroyers are the defensive workhorses of the fleet. Their traditional role is to detect and destroy, if possible, any threat to the fleet at a maximum distance from the main elements of the fleet. The role is not new but the methods are. When the major threat is air attack, destroyers are spread out as pickets to detect aircraft and engage them as early as possible. When the major threat is submarine attack, destroyers pull their ring of defense closer to the ships to be protected. The tighter defense is required because, compared to air weapons, submarine and antisubmarine weapons and detection means are all short range. As in most other aspects of naval warfare, the vicious undersea battle will be waged by underwater missiles designed especially for the purpose.

Escort ships. The escort ship (DE) is the smallest ship of a task force at sea. It is used as an antisub escort for hunter-killer groups, amphibious forces, and military convoys. The newest escorts will carry long-range sonar equipment and the drone antisubmarine helicopters. Asrocs and torpedoes are the primary armament. Although some escort ships (designated DEG) will have the Tartar missile for self defense against air attack, the primary mission of these ships is to protect escorted ships from submarine attack.

Submarines. With the introduction of guided missiles and nuclear energy, the military significance of the submarine is increasing more rapidly than that of any other naval vessel. Nuclear power dramatically extends the range and speed of submarines for, even with the necessarily heavy shielding, a nuclear propulsion system weighs less than the conventional engines, fuel tanks, and batteries. But the main advantages lie in the system's power and ability to operate without air, its lack of combustion products, and its negligible fuel requirements. The U. S. Navy's *Nautilus,* the first nuclear-powered submarine, was launched early in 1954 and now many others have followed.

Yet even before nuclear power and guided missiles, the submarine was a potent weapon. Submarines have sunk a greater tonnage of ships than all other war-making means put together. Before defeat of the German undersea fleet in World War II, millions of tons of shipping were lost, a hundred billion dollars had been expended, and a fourth of the scientific talent of the United States and Great Britain had been occupied with submarine defense.

Missiles and nuclear power have not been the only important recent developments in undersea warfare. The snorkel tube was built to decrease radar detection and still permit the submerged craft to draw air from the atmosphere. A tube the size of a barrel or less is far more difficult to locate than a submarine hull longer than a football field. High submerged speed has been made possible not only by modern propulsion, but by hull design as well. True submarines are replacing surface ships that merely were able to submerge. The new craft "fly" through the water using control vanes as does an airplane. Better food and oxygen supply allow modern nuclear submarines to stay at sea, submerged if necessary, for months at a time. For example, the USS *Triton* encircled the world submerged in 84 days.

The uses of submarines have been expanded considerably. The Japanese Navy built three large aircraft-carrying submarines during World War II and had planned to complete eighteen. These giants were 400 feet long and had a surface displacement of 5700 tons. The aircraft hangars each could hold four small seaplanes (one disassembled). Armament included a 105-mm or 140-mm gun, mounted aft of the hangar, and eight torpedo tubes. These remarkable ships could dive to 300 feet and had a 30,000-mile range. A modern counterpart could carry aircraft, troops, or cargo in substantial quantity.

Undersea craft have been used and will see increased use as troop transports, oilers, cargo carriers, rescue vessels, photo-reconnaissance and radar picket ships, and submarine killers. At least seventy Axis submarines were destroyed by Allied submarines in the last war, and modern developments indicate the necessity of "antisub" submarines. But the most dramatic and significant event in the history of submarine warfare occured in October 1949. During maneuvers off Hawaii, U. S. Navy submarines surfaced and fired modified V–1 guided missiles at the surface fleet far beyond the horizon. The missiles were deliberately guided past the fleet rather than directly at it, but the lethal warhead they could have carried might have spelled disaster for any ship. Eleven years later, the far more sophisticated Polaris missile broke the surface of the sea and blasted skyward in a high ballistic trajectory. This triumph came about, in large part, because a handful of dedicated submariners started with the old V–1 in 1949 and sold their idea to the Navy.

The submarine does have limited capacity compared to surface vessels, but new weapons, especially ASM's, will force increasing dependence upon the submersible combat vessel. The guided-missile submarine is a weapon of great strategic import.

Modern U. S. Navy submarines may be classified as conventional attack (SS), nuclear attack (SSN), and fleet ballistic missile (SSBN). The first category is still used because the older sub-

marines are available in substantial numbers and, with modernization, have a useful life of several more years.

Nuclear-attack submarines vary greatly in size and mission.
The first nuclear subs built, the *Nautilus* and the *Seawolf,* are essentially standard-hull-design, twin-propeller subs with nuclear
power plants. The second group have more advanced power plants
and hull design. One of them, the *Halibut,* is armed with the
Regulus, a turbojet-powered SSM. The third class is distinguished
by its size. The first of these, the *Triton,* is a radar picket ship and
one of the largest submarines ever built. It displaces 7750 tons
submerged and is powered by two nuclear reactors, each of which
is more powerful than the single reactors of the earlier subs.

The first completely new attack submarine, combining radical
new hull design, the latest nuclear propulsion, and detection
equipment, is the *Skipjack.* Designed primarily for submerged
operations, it is the fastest submarine ever built. A still later
version, a small nuclear-powered sub, will be used to hunt and
kill enemy subs. The *Tullibee* is one of this type. With a longer-
range sonar detection system than any other existing U. S. submarine, it is, in fact, an underwater fighter-intercepter.

The missile with which many of these subs will be armed is the
"Subroc" (submarine rocket). It fires from the torpedo tube, goes
to the surface, flies through the air, then reenters the water near
the enemy sub and attacks.

Conduct of Naval Operations

The United States must maintain freedom of the seas. By controlling sea areas, we can project military power overseas and we
can move quickly to new flare-ups of trouble if they are near the
seas—and much of the world's critical land area is near the seas.
By the use of naval forces we can relocate major elements of
military power without losing our investment in old bases, acquiring new bases, or encroaching on the sovereignty of other nations.

The very presence of naval forces may provide the solution to
the flare-up, as it did in the Formosa Straits. The inherent flexibility of naval forces to go to any part of the ocean and to almost

From the open sea, sudden attack. The Polaris missile breaks the surface above its submerged launcher. (Official U. S. Navy photograph.)

any shores on earth makes them a powerful cold- and limited-war force that we cannot afford to be without—and that, in time of war, an enemy cannot afford to tolerate.

Naval forces are deployed as fleets composed of carriers, cruisers, frigates, and destroyers; when required, they may have amphibious vessels, submarines, and supply vessels as well. These fleets project their power by employment of their weapons or by delivery and support of ground forces.

A naval fleet is a powerful offensive weapon system which constitutes such a threat that the enemy must eliminate it if he possibly can. He cannot attack with the big ballistic missiles, at least not with any hope of success. Naval forces are too elusive. Strategic missiles attack geographical coordinates—fixed targets—and the fleet is not fixed. The enemy's attack on the fleet will come from under the sea or from the air above it, direct gunnery attack by surface ships probably being a tactic of the past.

Defense against aircraft attack is met by a combination of means. First, the attack is detected as far out as possible by radar pickets, planes, submarines, or destroyers. Carrier-based fighter aircraft intercept first, destroying as many of the attackers as possible. They will deploy deadly heat-seeking Sidewinder or Sparrow air-to-air missiles. The Sidewinder is an ingeniously simple supersonic missile having no more electronic components than a small radio. It is 9 feet long, weighs 155 pounds, and uses an infrared homing device that causes it to "see" the target as a source of heat and head directly for it. The somewhat larger Sparrow is guided by a radar beam from the launching aircraft that can penetrate clouds and accurately find the target.

Those planes that penetrate the fighter defense will soon come within range of the ram-jet Talos missiles which are effective out to 65 miles or more. The Talos counters the ASM threat by reaching out to the probable range of launch with a nuclear warhead if required and attacking the launching aircraft. This potent killer is 30 feet long, weighs 3000 pounds, and travels well over twice the speed of sound.

Enemy planes surviving this defensive screen will find them-

Nuclear-tipped air-defense missiles guard the fleet. Talos missiles aboard the guided-missile cruiser USS "Galveston." (Official U. S. Navy photograph.)

selves coping with another defense, supersonic Terrier and Tartar guided missiles. The range of these high-kill-probability missiles is sufficient to attack a plane before it reaches the release point for a free-falling bomb. With such a formidable defense, the close-in attack by free-fall bombs or air-launched torpedoes costs more than the enemy will be willing to pay. He will resort to missile attack, launched by aircraft, surface ship, or submarines. The whole naval battle, offensive and defensive, promises to be a missile battle.

The submarine threat is even more serious than the airborne threat. The Soviet Union has more than 500 submarines. In the event of war many of these have the role of denying this coutry use of the seas, and some have the mission of launching nuclear missiles against the continental United States.

The United States must therefore have a strong antisubmarine defense. Antisubmarine warfare is a complex, costly, and extremely dangerous activity. Many different types of ships and devices are used including destroyers, submarines, mines (and the minecraft to lay them), aircraft (and the antisub carriers to launch them), helicopters, and blimps.

In the conduct of antisubmarine warfare, the U. S. Navy uses reconnaissance submarines to obtain information on enemy submarine and ship movements. Off our coasts the Navy maintains an aircraft patrol and sub hunter-killer groups consisting of an antisubmarine aircraft carrier, its aircraft, and destroyers. Submarine barriers are also established across potential transit routes. Hunter-killer groups join the various fleets for added antisub protection, move to likely areas of submarine activity, and escort military convoys.

Despite the development of air-to-surface missiles, guided torpedoes, and rocket-propelled depth charges, the most serious naval problem continues to be that of detecting the submerged enemy submarine. While submarines are vulnerable to detection by sonar, the detection range is limited. Underwater guided missiles are designed to permit accurate attack beyond sonar detection range, but underwater guidance systems have potential flaws too. Just as in air defense there is a see-saw of offense versus defense. Improved sonar detection equipment forces the enemy submarine to attack from a greater range, thus forcing him and the defender in turn to use longer-range weapons.

Does the Surface Fleet Have a Future?

A continuing controversy is the future of the surface fleet, particularly that of the big aircraft carrier. Will carriers and other surface vessels still be useful in the nuclear-missile and space age? Will they be able to survive? There is a vocal group of opponents who say no.

Consider first the carrier, the capital ship of today's fleet. Those opposed to further investment in the carrier say its current virtues are real indeed but for the future its limitations are very serious, particularly in nuclear warfare. Perhaps its major potential deficiency is the extreme vulnerability of the system. In another decade or less, aircraft, whatever their speed or altitude, will be so susceptible to missile interception that they will give way to missiles almost entirely. The handwriting is on the wall—or in the newspaper—when one reads that in 1960 a Nike-Hercules missile successfully intercepted a target traveling at more than three times the speed of sound and another at an altitude of over 150,000 feet. These are no isolated incidents, the Hercules has proved repeatedly that it can do this. Other missiles, including foreign ones, can perform similar feats. Therefore, the ballistic missile, submarine or land launched, will be the nuclear delivery means. An aircraft carrier is not needed, its opponents argue, if there are no aircraft to carry.

In a nuclear environment, the opponents add, the carrier is at least as vulnerable as its brood; probably more so, for the attack can be brought to the carrier, whereas an air-defense system has to wait for the planes to come to it. Enormous ocean areas can be searched by aircraft in a few hours. Modern airborne radar can detect a carrier hundreds of miles away, particularly if the carrier's search radar is operating. Once the carrier is located, nuclear-tipped ASM's or underwater guided missiles will distintegrate it with a direct hit. With a sufficiently potent warhead, even a gross miss will disable the target.

Another argument raised is that use of the large carrier violates a fundamental principle of war by its excessive concentration of combat power. The carrier is a dangerous weapon system from the enemy point of view. It must and will be eliminated whatever the cost; and the cost may not be too great, because carrier combat power will be concentrated in a few ships (their great expense and complexity dictating this limitation). In such a carrier is concentrated a substantial fraction of the total naval combat power which, once discovered, will never be lost to sight for there is no place to hide. Its low speed compared to aircraft makes it relatively immobile. Even submarines, when nuclear powered, potentially have comparable speed.

The surface-fleet opponent applies much of the same philosophy to other surface vessels, be they cruisers, destroyers, or transports. He insists that we must do with submersible ships everything that needs to be done at sea; the surface fleet is faced with extinction. These are powerful arguments, particularly difficult to discount if an unlimited nuclear war is visualized. But before we scrap the fleet, let us take another look at our need for surface forces, the vulnerability of aircraft, and the vulnerability of surface ships. First, the need.

The superiority of the submarine over the surface ship as a launching platform for ballistic missiles is immediately apparent. Yet the probability of an unlimited nuclear war appears low. If there is a low probability of nuclear war, we cannot rely solely on the effectiveness of submarines and ballistic missiles. We must be able to cope with the limited wars and threats of war as well.

The Navy's job in limited war is clear. In certain areas of the world the most simple and direct way to apply military power in the amount needed is by the use of naval forces. The action in the Formosa Straits is an example. The underdeveloped areas of the world are the most vulnerable to unrest, and many such areas are accessible to the sea. Virtually all of them are separated from the United States by the sea. When ground forces are required in these regions, naval forces have a vital role in their delivery and support.

But even in nuclear war, there remain missions to be accomplished at sea that perhaps only surface ships can perform. This nation is extremely vulnerable to missile-launching submarines; therefore, antisubmarine warfare will be a major undertaking. Today it appears that the best antisubmarine defense is accomplished by a combination of sea-based aircraft, destroyers, and submarines.

As for the vulnerability of aircraft and their probable replacement by missiles, this is indeed likely in nuclear war. The targets to be attacked by aircraft may be well protected by an air-defense system armed with nuclear missiles. But in limited war the converse is more probable. The scene of action more than likely will be an underdeveloped area where manpower is the most plentiful asset and where sophisticated air-defense systems are least in evidence. Even when a defense is in evidence, there is at times no substitute for the discriminating pilot who can use good judgment and act accordingly. The cost may be high, but it may be necessary to pay it.

The vulnerability of the carrier itself may not be as simple as described. The carrier need not be radiating any signals or radar to attract enemy attention. Other widely scattered ships, particularly submarines, can provide the radar early warning. Detection of "something at sea" must be followed by identification, too, and the modern fleet is going to make it very difficult for the patrol to close in and accomplish this.

Once the enemy has located and identified the carrier, however, he will press home his nuclear attack. It is difficult to imagine such a situation being anything but extremely grave. It must be conceded that a large target like a carrier, so easily distinguished from its background by "homing" missiles and so vulnerable to the nuclear warhead, has a low probability of survival in a determined nuclear attack. It may be that by completely preoccupying itself with defense, the carrier task force may postpone the almost inevitable outcome. But, if totally engrossed with defense, a surface fleet is of little positive value.

In the nonnuclear situation, the vulnerability problem is radically different. Modern carriers can sustain the damage of a considerable number of hits while exacting an awesome toll on the attackers.

In summation, it appears that the surface fleet is very much here to stay. While its offensive value is questionable in nuclear warfare, the surface fleet is of inestimable offensive value in limited war and in antisubmarine warfare under any circumstances. The surface fleet is particularly valuable as a limited-war weapon system, and limited war is the form of war most likely to appear for the next generation.

Future Warfare at Sea

To meet the demands of future nuclear warfare, as many combat ships as possible should be nuclear powered to ease fuel-supply problems and to increase range and independence of naval bases. They should also be submersible. Ideally, even transports and other support-type ships should be nuclear powered and submersible, but it may be mandatory for the combat vessel.

In a nuclear environment, offensive naval forces need to be able to move, hide, and move again, as army units do on land. The only way naval forces can do this is to submerge. They must be able to move unnoticed and to hide when the enemy is near, just as ground forces hide to avoid air attack. Defensive forces engaged in antisubmarine warfare, operating relatively close to friendly shores, can continue to use surface ships extensively.

Limited-warfare needs are quite different. Aircraft carriers will be used offensively in limited war far into the future. As air-defense systems and antiship missiles increase the vulnerability of both planes and their carriers, naval forces will place increasing emphasis on missiles as the primary weapons at sea. It is probable that aircraft carriers will then gradually phase into a primary role of surface transport for ground troops, their equipment, and their means of transportation. The amphibious assault ship is the first step in this direction. Carriers will probably always be mobile air-fields for manned combat aircraft as well, but this may very likely become their secondary role.

Future naval warfare will be characterized by extensive under-sea operations, as well as continued surface operations primarily in the conduct of antisubmarine warfare. Control of the seas will be dependent upon victory under the seas.

Surface transport will continue to be used wherever enemy action is so neutralized as to permit its reasonably safe operation. Economy and efficiency requirements dictate the mass use of surface shipping whenever feasible. A limited number of submersible transports should be available, however, for operation in hazardous areas.

Will the fleet survive in the nuclear age? Though severely taxed to defend itself against a myriad of missiles, it will not only survive but, with the addition of missile firepower of its own, will forge ahead with new offensive strength.

10. Strategic Missile Attack and Defense

"Soviet artillerymen, in the event of necessity, can with their rocket firepower support the Cuban people if the aggressive forces of the U. S. . . . ." Thus threatened Premier Khrushchev on the 9th of July 1960, while addressing the All-Russian Congress of Teachers in Moscow. He also reminded his listeners that Soviet artillery had a range of 13,000 kilometers (about 8100 miles).

The history of military technique has been dominated by efforts to improve firepower. In recent years developers have been spectacularly successful with that portion of firepower which we, like Khrushchev, may call artillery in a generic sense to differentiate it from short-range, close-combat firepower. Both the magnitude of this firepower and the means of delivery have made enormous strides in our time.

Since the beginning of armed conflict the warrior has tried to improve his ability to strike deep within an enemy fortress with minimum danger to himself and thus better support his assaulting troops. A succession of catapults, rockets, and guns led up to the Germans' famous "Paris Gun" of World War I which hurled a projectile 80 miles, but gun artillery was not practical at such a range.

The military airplane came along about that time and soon proved to be a better extension of conventional gun artillery. But here was a form of firepower that could be intercepted in flight, for it did not have the high-arching ballistic trajectory of artillery. It flew a relatively slow, level flight trajectory to the target, and had an airbreathing engine. To cope with this new form of firepower, anti-aircraft artillery and intercepter aircraft were developed and thus aerial warfare evolved.

Then, with World War II, came a technological breakthrough and the beginning of a return to ballistic-trajectory artillery, this time rocket propelled. The German Army revealed it first with the 200-mile-range V–2 rocket. Here again was artillery power which at that time could not be intercepted in flight.

To prevent its being fired was equally difficult. Nearly 1500 Allied fliers lost their lives in aircraft raids on V–weapon launching sites, but this new artillery could not be adequately countered. The firing batteries were too mobile and easily hidden. The Americans used to sit in their foxholes in the front lines in Western Europe during the winter of 1944–1945 and watch those rockets being fired in the night far ahead in enemy territory and falling somewhere far to their rear. What a feeling of utter helplessness it was to know that, in spite of their superiority on the ground and in the air, the only solution was to seize the enemy's territory and deny him the area he needed to be within V–2 striking range of London and Antwerp. Only the lack of a nuclear warhead, which missiles now have, prevented this serious harassment from bringing disaster to the Allies.

The Germans' other approach to artillery firepower, the V–1 buzz bomb, was actually a pilotless aircraft. But because it had the level-flight characteristics of an airplane, is was highly vulnerable to antiaircraft artillery fire and intercepters. The V–1 weapons were shot down by the thousands.

After World War II the advantages of strategic artillery power, in the form of long-range ballistic missiles, became obvious to all. Still, because of the many technological hurdles to be overcome and the uncertainty of the date of operational readiness of ICBM's, nations have continued to depend upon more conventional techniques developed in air warfare.

Yet missiles are rendering the very term *air warfare* obsolete. A few years ago the full impact of missiles on aerial combat could not be predicted, for there were many technological uncertainties. But now it appears that, after a transitional period during which bomber aircraft will continue to predominate, air warfare will almost cease to exist. The air will be but a thin crust through

New possibilities for the manned bomber? Artist's conception of the RS–70 Valkyrie, intercontinental supersonic aircraft.

which missile artillery will flash in seconds at the beginning and end of its ballistic trajectory. This does not necessarily mean the end of the manned bomber. There will probably always be some specialized combat roles for bombers. Manned weapon systems of the future may also be able to rise above the atmosphere. However, before we analyze this era, let us examine the weapons of the transitional period.

Offensive Air Operations

The ability of air weapons to attack targets from another continent brought about greater emphasis in the 1950's on air offense and air defense than on any other form of combat. Now fleets of bombers and nests of air-defense missiles stand poised on opposite sides of the oceans in one great threat and stalemate of action.

Piloted bombers. Let us examine the characteristics of these bombers. Obviously, strategic bombers should have the range necessary for the task, the ability to accomplish the attack mission after reaching the target area, and the means to protect themselves from attack while en route. The basic problem in obtaining these characteristics is that of properly combining speed, range, armament, and payload. Improvement of each of these four factors tends to be at the expense of the other three.

But modern bombers are gradually improving in all respects. Consider, for example, the jet aircraft known as the RS–70 "Valkyrie." This planned weapon system, if developed would be the first truly intercontinental supersonic manned weapon system. At 70,000 feet it would fly at three times the speed of sound, and it has a design range of 6000 miles without refueling. The Canard-design (control surfaces forward) giant would be 200 feet long and, with its huge delta wing aft, would look more like a monster dart than an airplane. It would be powered by a row of six jet engines clustered in the tail.

Proponents of the Valkyrie point out that the United States will need a reconnaissance and strike aircraft for at least ten years and possibly longer. Besides, it has other valuable qualities. In a cargo configuration it could carry eighty combat troops almost anywhere in the world faster than the movement of the sun. With its high speed and altitude ceiling, it could be used as a retrievable first-stage booster for earth satellites. In a peacetime role it offers intercontinental supersonic passenger service.

Yet with all the speed and range of such aircraft of the near future, they are worthless if their payload cannot hit the intended targets. Even when the bombardier uses nuclear weapons, accuracy is important. It is a fallacious theory that a weapon which is effective over a large area can be dropped anywhere within that area. Certainly the most outstanding limitation of the conventional unguided aircraft bomb is its lack of accuracy when dropped from high altitude. Satisfactory accuracy can be achieved only by close-in attacks without prohibitive losses. What is the solution? The air-to-surface missile.

The military value of a bomber will be increased many times if it can release its payload a great distance from the target without sacrificing accuracy. The ASM capable of meeting this need will require fewer flights and far less tonnage of bombs dropped to accomplish a particular mission.

Air-to-surface missiles. These missiles can be classified as controlled gravity bombs, glide bombs, and powered missiles. The first two are primarily of historical value; modern air-defense missiles make their use against a defended target too dangerous. Modern tactics demand a missile that can be launched from beyond the reach of the defense.

The powered missile is the third and modern ASM. The weapon has its own propulsion system and can fly a considerable distance after being launched. An outstanding World War II example of this type was the air-launched German V–1 missile. More than 150 miles from London, the target, German bombers dropped the V–1, which then carried its 2000-pound warhead under its own power. The modern version now under development is the U. S. Air Force "Skybolt." The characteristics of this air-launched ballistic missile (ALBM) are still secret but, because the carrier plane can fire it at a target from a point beyond the reach of the target's defenses, the Skybolt promises to extend the useful life of manned bombers.

Air-to-surface missiles are most effective against ships, bridges, structures, and other targets easily distinguished from their backgrounds, because automatic target-seeking devices can then be used. They are particularly valuable against well-defended targets, since their increased range permits launching beyond the range of air-defense weapons. Some potential disadvantages of ASM's are their lack of accuracy against targets not easily distinguished, their complexity and extra space requirements, and the vulnerability of the ASM's themselves to the defense. However, against certain targets these disadvantages may well be outweighed by the advantages.

An aerial striking arm equipped with fast long-range jet bombers

Modern ASM. The Skybolt, now under development, will permit the bomber carrying it to attack from 1000 miles away. (Official U. S. Air Force photograph.)

and armed with ASM's must retain a high priority until the strategic missile force fully matures. But if the enemy is capable of producing the same weapon, what defense is there against such a force?

The Air-Defense Problem

The margin of safety once provided by time and distance is constantly being reduced. The enemy bomber force is only a few hours away, regardless of its location anywhere on earth, and we must have a defense against this form of attack. There are two fundamental approaches to air defense, equally important and necessary. One is to protect critical areas with an efficient air-defense system, and the other is to build an offensive air arm capable of attacking the enemy force at its source. Neither of these methods can be neglected.

The concept has been advanced that there is no adequate solution to the air-defense problem and that the only certain way for a nation to stop strategic bombardment is to engage in strategic bombardment. This school of thought includes the premise that if two warring nations have strategic air forces, the first target for each is the other's ability to employ those forces. Once the victor of that conflict is decided, destruction by strategic bombardment can be controlled, and the total destruction caused by the war may even be lessened. General Hoyt S. Vandenberg, former U. S. Air Force Chief of Staff, once observed, "The whole proof of defense against an enemy power is attrition and destruction on the other end."

The strategic capability contributes greatly to air defense, but it is not in itself sufficient. It is certainly true that a total defensive attitude is fatal in warfare, but air defense should not be discarded as useless. On the contrary, the defense is enormously improved by the guided missile.

Any air-defense system devised suffers inherent handicaps. The most important disadvantage of the defense is that the attacker has the initiative. The offense has the choice of time, place, and means of attack. The defense can act only when the aggressor has initiated an attack. It follows, then, that one of the biggest problems in air defense is to discover the attack at the earliest possible moment. Of course, there are technical difficulties in the solution of this problem. For example, radar has the shortcomings of inability to distinguish friend from foe, susceptibility to interference, and inability to cope with the curvature of the earth (since radar energy travels in a straight line). Other means are necessary for identification. It may even be necessary to control rigidly all friendly civilian and military air traffic. Then, when an unidentified plane appears where it is not supposed to be, it is shot down. This is severe treatment for a erring friendly pilot, but there may be no alternative.

Despite the complexity of problem, air defense has many points in its favor. With an efficient early-warning system, it can detect approaching aircraft in time to counter their attack. Although bombers have an almost infinite number of routes to a high-priority target, they must approach it ultimately and expose themselves to attack. This defensive attack will not be merely a token effort, for modern air-defense weapons have reached a high level of effectiveness. Although strategically on the defensive, missiles and intercepter aircraft are tactically on the offensive and may well inflict staggering losses on a bomber force.

An adequate air-defense weapons system should consist of both long-range intercepter aircraft carrying AAM's, and surface-to-air missiles. Consider first the intercepter.

Intercepters and air-to-air missiles. The long-range intercepter should be a fast, all-weather fighter with sufficient range to meet the enemy far from the target area. The long range also permits intercepters at widely scattered bases to be mutually supporting. The intercepter should be armed exclusively with guided rockets and be semiautomatic in operation. But why the rockets?

It was stated in Chapter 2 that as bombers and fighters approach and exceed sonic velocity, aerial combat with conventional guns becomes almost impossible. If both planes are flying 1000 miles per hour toward each other, their relative velocity is 2000 miles per hour. This means that if the pilot were so fortunate as even to see his adversary a mile away, two seconds later he would have passed him. He would be within gun range for less than half a second. A right-angle approach is equally futile because the target is in the line of fire only an instant. To turn into the bomber in a pursuit curve is no good either until the fighter is actually on the tail of the bomber, because at high speed the radius of turn is so great that the bomber is never within range. Of course, once the intercepter is on the bomber's tail, gunnery will be effective if the fighter is close enough and the target can be seen; but that is also the time when the fighter is most vulnerable to the tail guns of the bomber.

The fighter could carry free (unguided) rockets to fire a large volume of lethal projectiles in the shortest possible time. Yet even with free rockets the high-speed intercepter, flying at an altitude of 50,000 feet or more, not only has an extremely short time of interception with an enemy bomber but doubtless will have no opportunity to make more than one or two passes. Modern aircraft also are more rugged than their predecessors and must receive direct or near hits to be brought down.

The air-to-air guided missile is the only answer for piloted intercepters. Once launched, the robot projectile streaks forward at several times the speed of sound, automatically flying an interception course.

Fighters are not necessarily the only aircraft that will use AAM's. Bombers also may be armed with these new weapons and thus increase their ability to fight their way through intercepters to distant targets. But the AAM is of more advantage to the fighter than to the bomber. Not having the heavy fuel and bomb load that the bomber does, the fighter can devote nearly all available space to missiles and electronic equipment to guide them; but the bomber must sacrifice bomb load or range to carry an appreciable number of AAM's. Of course, it is entirely possible that some planes could be equipped mostly with missiles, having as their primary mission protection of the bombers.

The air-to-air missile is not without limitations. The pilot must still find and close on the target before attacking. Even with ground-radar control this is sometimes difficult. The size and weight of the AAM limits the number of missiles that can be carried. The requirement for smaller size necessitates miniaturization of all components without loss of performance or reliability. To launch a missile laterally or rearward is desirable, but serious stability problems must be solved first. It is such problems as these that the tactician sometimes overlooks.

Surface-to-air missiles. The most certain method of destroying an enemy bomber is to fire at it a guided missile that not only has great speed, range, and lethality but also the ancillary equipment necessary to detect the target in time to act. This weapon is the surface-to-air missile.

Surface-to-air missiles are propelled by either rocket motors or ram jets. In general, rocket propulsion systems are preferable for shorter-range missiles, and ram jets are more practical at long range. Compared with an antiaircraft gun, the SAM is characterized by a large warhead, greatly increased range, and a high probability of destroying the target with a single round. Gun artillery could cope only with aircraft flying half the speed of sound (under 40,000 feet) and expended thousands of rounds of ammunition for each plane destroyed. The Nike-Ajax can reach out 25 miles and knock down supersonic aircraft up to 60,000 feet with a 90 percent probability of success. The Nike-Hercules can more than double its little brother's performance in every respect and destroy tactical ballistic-missile targets, such as the Corporal, as well. The Air Force ram-jet "Bomarc" can reach out more than 200 miles.

For effective air defense, guided missiles and intercepter aircraft must be coordinated into a single air-defense system. Eventually an all-missile defense system may eliminate the use of aircraft entirely. One can easily visualize the intricate early-warning and target-identification system that will be necessary in this integrated air defense. It must have great detection range, and it must be almost completely automatic in operation. The United States air defense includes two such systems, one for local control and one for regional control. The local, nicknamed "Missile Master," coordinates up to several dozen batteries in one metropolitan-area defense. The regional system, "Sage," controls longer-range air-breathing missiles and manned intercepters.

Ballistic Missiles

After the indeterminate transitional period in which both the manned bomber and the long-range missile will have intercontinental artillery roles, it appears that the strategic bomber will give way almost entirely to the ballistic missile. In strategic missile warfare, the intercontinental ballistic missile (ICBM), intermediate-range ballistic missile (IRBM), and submarine-launched intracontinental missile (SLIM) would play the major roles. The SLIM is particularly important; as a component of strategic missile operations the submarine-launched missile is difficult to intercept in flight and its mobile launcher is equally difficult to counter.

The heavyweight of this missile trio is the ICBM. To attain intercontinental range, the ICBM will initially climb steeply into space and consume all of its propellant simply to get above the atmosphere. Following a great-circle arc, it will glide powerless a thousand or more miles high before starting its descent. Once the missile is free of the drag of air, its range is limited only by its velocity (10,000 to 15,000 miles per hour). By the use of multistage rockets (whereby a missile fires a smaller rocket from its nose when its own fuel is exhausted, the smaller rocket launches still another, and so on), the range can be extended as far as desired. Thus the ICBM could well be sent the "long way around" to reach the target.

Will the ICBM, IRBM, and SLIM replace the bomber? The arguments favoring missile artillery over the manned bomber are now well known. Today the bomber is the major nuclear delivery means, but its effectiveness is decreasing because it is so vulnerable to air-defense missiles. The time will soon come when any air-breathing craft, regardless of speed or altitude, can be shot down by rocket-powered air-defense missiles that can always be designed beyond any given speed or altitude ceiling.

Speed of delivery too favors the missile over the bomber. The much higher speed of the missile gives the defender minimum warning and a far more difficult target to intercept.

Even cost probably gives the nod to the missile, as expensive as it may seem. A bomber making a long-range bombing raid must sacrifice bomb load to carry a crew and sufficient fuel to return to its base. The guided missile is a one-way aircraft stripped of all the crew, armament, pressurized cabin, landing gear, and other such "nonessentials." Consider the relative cost of piloted plane and missile. For a given bomb load, accuracy, and range, the guided missile will be much smaller than the plane and will cost, in mass production, perhaps one-tenth as much to build and launch. If the average combat life of a bomber were ten missions, to use it would be no more economical than to fire ten missiles. Therefore, it can be seen, even disregarding the value of human lives, that missiles may become cheaper for the attacker if the air defense inflicts losses on the bombers in excess of 10 percent per raid. Such an attrition rate on the enemy is quite possible, and it may even be much higher with SAM battalions added to the defense. This comparison is oversimplified but the principle is valid. This situation forces the use of long-range ballistic missiles.

Shifting the weight of emphasis to the missile does not, however, mean elimination of the bomber. A limited number of manned aircraft will always be essential. A few bombers should be retained, if for no other reason than to force the enemy to maintain an expensive air-defense system. A manned system will be able to obtain intelligence and damage-assessment information that no unmanned system can duplicate. Bombers can attack mobile targets and targets of opportunity more readily than missiles, and they can achieve higher accuracy with poor target data. The human pilot offers distinct advantages. He can employ a wide range of tactics, use his judgment to cope with unexpected situations, disregard targets already destroyed and use his weapons on alternate targets. He can think, observe, and make decisions.

Yet overshadowing these advantages is the increasing effectiveness of air-defense systems. Consequently bombers should be reserved for specialized missions that missiles cannot accomplish. It appears that there will always be such missions and the bomber, though having only a minor role, will never become extinct. Who can tell but that some day ballistic-missile defense will become so effective that the manned bomber, then in space, will reestablish the pilot's ascendancy in strategic attack?

Of the various strategic ballistic missiles on the scene today, the two most promising and most certain to have a low obsolescence rate are the Minuteman and the Polaris.

The Minuteman is a three-stage solid-propellant ICBM which will have a maximum range of at least 5500 miles. For the missile to obtain this range, the third stage will have a maximum speed

Solid-propellant ICBM. A full-scale, flight-weight, silo-test model of the Air Force Minuteman is pictured on its transporter enroute to the launch site. (Official U. S. Air Force photograph.)

of more than 15,000 miles per hour. The inertial-guidance system is expected to deliver its nuclear warhead with amazing accuracy, considering the great distance it must go.

The Minuteman may be called a second-generation missile because it incorporates so many improvements over the huge liquid-propellant Atlas and Titan, mainstays of today's ICBM force. The missile is small enough to be transported by truck, train, or even aircraft. It will be fired both from underground blastproof silos and could be fired from rail mobile launchers. Once set up and checked out, the missile will be ready to fire on a moment's notice; the designers are emphasizing simplicity. The Minuteman will require very little supporting equipment and will be able to stand by, ready to fire, for long periods of time with little maintenance. If these missiles were deployed on trains they would be able to move secretly from time to time and set up on new sites so that location and counterattack by the enemy would be extremely difficult.

The Polaris (model A–1) is a first-generation, two-stage, solid-propellant missile designed primarily for firing from submarines, specially designed for the weapon. When fired, the missile is ejected vertically from the submarine, either submerged or surfaced, by inert gases that boost it clear of the water. Then the first-stage rocket motor ignites, and the 1200-mile-range missile is on its way.

Despite the fact that the Polaris submarine is not anchored to a geodetic triangulation point, it has a remarkable ability to locate itself with respect to the target and fire with great accuracy. The secret is its SINS (Ship's Inertial Navigation System). This precision device continuously and automatically determines the submarine's geographical coordinates. All movements of the submarine, for any reason, are sensed and recorded. In addition, navigational "fixes" can be obtained by several other means, including navigation satellites such as the "Transit."

Like the Minuteman, the inertially guided Polaris follows the path of a projectile; hence it is called a ballistic missile. Sixteen missiles are carried on each submarine, and construction of forty-one nuclear-powered Polaris-firing submarines is planned. Once operational, each submarine loads its deadly ammunition and disappears into the seas on its mission of deterrence. By the use of two crews for each submarine, the Navy will be able to keep a high percentage of the missile launchers on patrol continuously. The next generation of Polaris, a 1500-mile missile designated the A–2, is already fully developed.

In the United States the transition from bombers to missiles has already begun with the deployment of liquid-propellant IRBM's (Jupiter and Thor), ICBM's (Atlas and Titan), and solid-propellant submarine-launched missiles (Polaris). However, we urgently need to move on, as indeed we are doing, to more advanced

Mission: strategic missile attack. The ballistic-missile submarine USS "George Washington" under way in the Atlantic. (Official U. S. Navy photograph.)

systems. Our land-based missiles are tied to fixed launching emplacements which invite disaster. The huge liquid-propellant ICBM sites are necessarily fixed for technical reasons, but IRBM's should be fired from completely mobile launchers and supported by mobile ground equipment.

As soon as feasible, the ground-based liquid-propellant IRBM's and Polaris A–1's should be replaced by an 1800-mile-range submarine-launched intracontinental missile (SLIM). The Navy is already developing such a missile; the Polaris A–3 will have a 2500-mile range. By using launching points in the coastal areas of a continent, the SLIM can reach any target within the continent. The combination of nuclear-powered undersea mobility and underwater launching without warning from almost anywhere makes it virtually immune to countermeasures. Even if the enemy could detect and attack these launchers, the battle would be at sea, not in the midst of our homeland. When fully developed, this system will become a major component of the nation's strategic attack capability.

The next phase-in should be the solid-propellant ICBM with mobile launching site and ground equipment. Mobile Minuteman squadrons, like the SLIM carriers, should be dispersed and moved at random from time to time so that enemy location and neutralization of more than a fraction of the total would be impossible. Why both the ICBM and the SLIM? Both have limitations, but different limitations; in combination they present a far more difficult problem to the enemy.

What developments beyond these? Possibly, as eventual replacements for the Atlas and Titan, a solid-propellant missile still bigger than the Minuteman and a space bomber, such as that discussed in Chapter 11, should come into the inventory.

The SSM-Defense Problem

Now let us consider the problem of an enemy guided-missile "strategist" planning a nuclear attack on the United States. Visualize his studying the approaches to the industrial centers of the country from the Eurasian continent. A cursory examination of a global map will reveal that American cities are not easy to reach from Eurasia. Pittsburgh is 3600 miles away from the closest point in Western Europe. The distance from the eastern tip of Siberia to Southern California with its defense industries is more than 3000 miles. This is why 5000-mile missiles are needed to reach all of North America. Of course, the Soviets have clearly demonstrated by the Pacific firings that they have such missiles—indeed, the ability to attack the "long" way around the world—but the great distance involved does give us some warning time and does tend to diminish the accuracy of the attack.

Our hypothetical attacker could employ launching sites at sea. Any potential target in the United States is within 1200 miles of the sea. What warning could we expect from a submarine-launched attack? Perhaps fifteen minutes at most.

A popular cry is that there is no defense against intercontinental missile artillery, but this is simply not so. Many of the same passive means of defense that are used against bombers may be employed. The defense should disperse critical installations, construct protective shelters, confuse homing-type missiles with dummy targets or electronic jamming, and establish an efficient missile-attack warning service.

By these means alone, population losses from massive nuclear attack on the United States could be reduced to perhaps a tenth or less of the losses that would be suffered without such protection. Most important, mere existence of these passive means would help to deter attack because the potential attacker would know that his assault could not be decisive.

Unfortunately, too little is being done in the United States about two of these means. There is little industry or population dispersion, and few missile-defense shelters. An example of what can be done is seen in the new plant of the Stanford Research Institute at Palo Alto, California. The basement of one of the buildings is a shelter for 3000 persons, and building plans include another basement to shelter 2000 more. The cost of survival shelters? Another 5 percent added to total cost, and no loss of peacetime usefulness for the rooms so designed. Home fallout-protection shelters can be built for as little as $50 and combined blast and fallout shelters for as little as $500.

But there are active means of defense also. They are admittedly more difficult to achieve than passive defense but just as important. Why so difficult?

The ballistic-missile launching base can be anywhere on earth, or even under the sea, and the missile can be fired directly toward the target or the long way around the earth in a near-orbital trajectory. It will rise a thousand or more miles above the earth and descend toward the target at 4 miles per second. By the time the atmosphere begins to slow it down, it will probably have cast off all firing stages and will consist only of a small warhead glowing from the heat or friction.

This is the target that must be countered. An active defense against it is vital because of the missile threat now developing. The Soviet Union is reported to be building a major strategic rocket force which has received such emphasis that it is now a separate branch of the Soviet armed forces. This force is particularly significant because at the present time there is no active defense against it; we are faced with an intolerable military situation. Our policy as a peace-loving nation is to refuse to initiate a "preventive" nuclear attack. Today we are therefore obliged to accept, without defense, the first nuclear-missile blow by the enemy. A missile-defense system is an urgent military need.

Moreover, it is important that the United States be in the position of having an adequate missile defense first. The nation in this position may upset the balance of mutual deterrence and, if inclined to aggression, with its reduced vulnerability it may be tempted to attack.

There are four phases in the life of a strategic ballistic missile during which it may be attacked. It may be destroyed (1) on the ground or at sea before it is launched, (2) during the initial powered stage of flight, (3) while it coasts through space in the middle portion of its trajectory, or (4) during the terminal phase of flight as it reenters the atmosphere and approaches its intended target. Each of these four periods must be thoroughly explored and reexplored with advancing technology to uncover any feasible solutions to defense.

Destruction of the missile during the first phase, the prelaunch period, is the classic artillery "counterbattery-fire" approach, complicated by modern developments. An artillery counterattack on the hostile batteries of artillery to prevent their firing is a historical solution that still has promise if the missile batteries can be located. The size and complexity of first-generation ICBM's and their ground support do render them vulnerable to counterattack. Unfortunately, as time passes, missiles will become increasingly difficult to find before they are launched. With the advent of solid-propellant strategic missiles, the enemy can make his launchers mobile and move them at random throughout his land or under the sea. Such mobility may make prelaunch detection and location extremely difficult, but the apparent difficulty must not preclude the search for solutions or development of means to attack when the enemy missile sites can be found.

The second phase, the initial powered stage of flight, may prove to be an effective time to intercept an ICBM in flight. It is moving relatively slowly, taking no evasive action, and revealing itself clearly by its long bright tail of flame. But our defense would have to be immediately available; the means to attack the rising ICBM may have to be space based in order to respond fast enough. Infrared homing rockets could be mounted on orbiting space bases and launched as the missiles are detected rising above the atmosphere. This solution requires major advances in technology, particularly in development of orbital launching platforms, and will necessitate the use of many orbiting platforms to cover all potential launching areas on earth. Nevertheless, the concept should be pursued aggressively until its true feasibility is determined. Certainly one indication of feasibility is the Soviet Venus rocket, which was launched in a highly precise manner from its orbiting platform. The rocket could just as easily be designed for other targets. In cooperation with the Advanced Research Projects Agency (ARPA) of the Department of Defense, the U. S. Air Force is conducting research to establish the feasibility of such a system.

The third phase in the life of an ICBM, its mid-trajectory transit of space, appears to offer the least promise for defense. The missile is moving very high and very fast; is has no exhaust and creates no detectable disturbance in space. Yet there it coasts for perhaps fifteen to thirty minutes in a fixed predictable trajectory. Surely research pointed at neutralization during this phase is justified.

Clearly the most promising phase for interception, with existing technology, is the last. No matter where the missile is launched or what unusual trajectory it follows, it must come to the target where the defense waits for it. Since the defender is attacking the incoming missile during the final phase of flight, he has maximum warning time. The terminal trajectory is predictable and the interception problem is not difficult to solve. A terminal defense system also takes advantage óf existing technology. Air-defense systems already developed have proven their ability to hit shorter-range ballistic missiles. An extrapolation of current systems can provide the earliest solution; this is an important feature, for the threat is almost upon us.

The Advanced Research Projects Agency is carefully studying all phases of ICBM flight for long-range solutions to defense against them. Under ARPA project Defender more than $200 million has been invested in ballistic-missile defense.

In addition to its advanced research program, the United States is rapidly approaching an immediate solution to missile defense. The Army, capitalizing on the advantages of a terminal defense and Army experience in air defense, has developed and will soon test its Nike-Zeus system. The need for a missile defense was anticipated after World War II, but it was not until 1955 that serious "hardware" development began on the Nike-Zeus. Just how effective this system can be will be determined by tests in the Pacific. At Kwajalein the Army is installing a complete Nike-Zeus complex for full system tests against actual ICBM's. At Vandenberg Air Force Base in California, more than 4000 miles away, the Air Force will fire the target missiles.

Let us look at how the Zeus system works. It employs the same guidance and propulsion principles as its predecessors, the Nike-

Ajax and Nike-Hercules. First the Zeus acquisition radar scans an enormous volume of space in all directions to detect, hundreds of miles away, any incoming missiles. This radar has two components: a transmitter that sweeps the sky with a signal, and a huge focusing receiver to detect any reflection of the signal. Once a target is acquired, a second radar, called the discrimination radar, begins to follow it and supply the precise data needed for attack. This radar is designed to distinguish the real warhead from decoys or any other false targets the ICBM might eject to confuse the defense.

Now the warhead is accurately identified, plunging thousands of miles per hour toward its target, and the time for counterattack has come. Two additional radars go into action, one to track the incoming missile and one to track the Zeus missile. Both tracking radars automatically feed information into a computer which solves the interception problem. At the precise time desired, a Zeus missile is fired and the computer controls it all the way to interception. When the Zeus closes for the kill, the computer dictates the instant of detonation and the ICBM warhead is destroyed. The entire operation is automatic and takes place in seconds. The system is so designed in such a way that many Zeus missiles can be in the air at the same time without conflict.

The Nike-Zeus is a three-stage solid-propellant missile, the best and only defense that the nation can produce today. An indication of the power and size of the missile is the 450,000-pound thrust of the first stage, the most powerful solid-propellant rocket motor in the United States. The Zeus enthusiasts also like to point out its growth potential as a space-defense system to attack hostile satellites.

What are the advantages of an early deployment of the Zeus system? First it provides, at nominal cost, the only possible defense for the near future. Cost is important; a desirable feature of any defense is that it not consume a disproportionate share of the total military effort. The cost of establishing an effective defense of key national centers would be about a billion dollars a year over a six- to eight-year period, about what we would spend for cigarettes in

For every offense a defense. The antimissile Nike-Zeus hurtles toward space and the incoming missile. (U. S. Army photograph.)

the United States during the same period. But the cost comparison that really needs to be made is the relative damage to the nation with and without a defense. Is anything more expensive than widespread destruction and losing the war?

Another advantage of having an operational Zeus system is that it complicates the enemy attack. With a U. S. defense in operation the enemy attack problem is greatly aggravated, possibly even insoluble. He is forced to resort to complicated and expensive countermeasures in an attempt to neutralize the defense. He will know that some countermeasures, such as decoys, will not be effective against the Nike-Zeus defense. He must increase many times the number of missiles he fires to assure hits. Even then he has no guarantee of complete success—and if he attacks, he dare not fail to be completely successful.

The Nike-Zeus also adds to deterrence against attack. Deterrence, after all, is a state of mind and any means of diminishing the effectiveness of the attack reinforces this state of mind. Most important of all, should rash judgment, an irrational mind, or an accidental firing precipitate an attack in spite of our efforts, we must be able to counter it.

It is probable, of course, that the Nike-Zeus defense will not provide 100 percent assurance of protection. A perfect ICBM defense is far from being a reality, especially a defense against a massive simultaneous attack. Yet the nation should not sit unprotected for lack of a perfect defense. A soccer team does not eliminate its goalie because the opposing team occasionally gets the ball past him.

The alternative of no defense is the truly dangerous and expensive course of action. Without a defense to complicate his tactics, the enemy has a simple problem of conducting an unopposed attack with a high assurance of success.

The Total War

A common image of total war is a sudden exchange of nuclear-tipped missiles which create such vast destruction on both sides that within a few hours, or days at most, one belligerent or the other must surrender. This is a grossly oversimplified and even erroneous view of total war, for it fails to take cognizance of many factors and unknowns involved. Total war covers a much broader scope of effort than an initial nuclear attack. The outcome of a total war will probably hinge upon many succeeding clashes of forces in many environments and over an extended period of time.

Total war includes not only strategic missile attack, but also strategic bomber attack; defense against such attacks; survival and recuperation; movement across the seas; invasion, seizure, and control of the enemy heartland; and elimination of the opponent's will to resist. Each of these elements may vary in form and importance at any given time. Thus many variations of action and counteraction are possible.

To deter total war, the United States should present the enemy with such a convincing ability to withstand attack and to defeat the attacker that he will never risk it. Our military posture must be of such adaquacy and so well balanced that when the enemy has considered all the factors, planned for contingencies, and weighed all the variations possible, he will always arrive at the decision not to attack.

Surely the problem is more complicated than where the "missile gap" lies. Let us hypothesize that two great nations on separate continents suddenly become engulfed in total war—war in which national survival is at stake and no tools of war are withheld. Both have powerful strategic missile attack forces, active and passive defenses, ground and naval forces, air and sea transportation, and will to win.

Now let us vary one of these factors and visualize the results. Assume, for example, that neither side has missile-defense shelters or an active missile defense. The results of a massive exchange under these circumstances almost defy description. Great fiery explosions would blossom in dozens of large governmental, industrial, military, and population centers, and invisible shadows of lethal radiation would stretch downwind tens and hundreds of miles from each burst. Some targets, deliberately "saved" for postwar use, might experience only the lethal but nondestructive radiation.

Within a few days the death toll could become a major percentage of both nations and within a few weeks could well exceed half of both. Out of this senseless carnage and destruction would come paralysis on both sides. With destruction and death so widespread, attention to saving what is left would become paramount.

Would the war be over? Possibly, but not necessarily. The residual capability of a nation to fight on, even though badly hurt, has been too well demonstrated in history to disregard now. The Pyrrhic victory could well be won by the antagonist who managed to constitute an assault force and transportation enough to invade the enemy's land, destroy any remaining element of resistance, and assume control of what was left. The conflict could even be won by a third nation which did not attack until the first two had reduced themselves to military impotence. These are just some of the possibilities—and we have varied only one element, the defense against strategic attack. The prospect of a thermonuclear exchange, particularly with a low level of defense, is so terrifying that we must ask ourselves whether there is any alternative to such madness. The logical alternative is to abandon these means entirely; but if a major power threatens the United States with such attack, there is no choice but to have adequate power. Thus does the modern world find itself in a nervous stalemate of mutual deterrence.

Suppose we reinstate an effective defense element and again imagine the results. It is immediately apparent that the destruction and particularly the death toll would be dramatically reduced. Herman Kahn, in his book, *On Thermonuclear War*, estimates that with an effective passive defense alone, casualties can be reduced from 60 to 90 percent.

Thus the initial attack is even less decisive and the other elements of war assume even greater importance. There is an almost endless variety of possibilities within this set of assumptions. What if one side decides to concentrate on cities and the other on opposing military forces? What if one belligerent withholds a substantial portion of his firepower for contingencies and the other does not?

Now let us vary the defense factor again: give one nation an effective defense and the other little or none. The results would be so lopsided, the victory so obviously in the hands of the nation with a defense, that an aggressive nation with this advantage might even attempt to dictate its own peace terms without firing a missile.

Throughout this simplified analysis we have varied only one factor—defense—and held the others constant. Variations of the other factors, one at a time, will produce startling results too, and multiple variations still more startling results. Clearly, the image of total war is not a simple picture that can be framed with a dogmatic solution; such a solution would likely be the one Mencken described as neat, plausible, and wrong.

Push Buttons and Manpower

There is a tendency on the part of some to minimize the importance of the human element in a future war. A prominent writer one stated that "automatic warfare cancels out the importance of human qualities except in passive form." Surely some basic facts were not recognized when this premise was advanced. It is now normal procedure to launch missiles rather than aircraft for some missions. But the most important link of all, man, is till there. He operates by remote control or by the use of prearranged navigation he inserted before the missile was launched. All of the crew chiefs, armorers, mechanics, electronic and propulsion technicians are still there too.

In summary, the primary weapon for strategic attack will be the missile. This does not necessarily mean that the manned bomber should be abandoned entirely. Certainly no missile can duplicate the ability of the airman to reason and use good judgment. But piloted aircraft—any air-breathing craft at any speed—may be so vulnerable to defensive missiles that their use will prove prohibitively costly. Great air battles by opposing fleets of planes will be as obsolete as the cavalry charge. Aerial combat between piloted aircraft will be almost impossible, because the speeds and accelerations necessary for survival will be beyond human endurance.

Guided missiles will add greatly to air defense and virtually eliminate air warfare itself. The air-to-air missile will increase the capability of intercepters until surface-to-air missiles replace intercepters entirely. The day will come when air space will be controlled by the force that controls the ground or sea beneath it.

Although intercontinental offensive striking power eventually will be provided by ballistic missiles, a strategic air force will continue to be the primary means of delivery for several years. The strategic air arm acts as a powerful deterrent to enemy attack because of its retaliatory power and must be retained in strength until an adequate quantity of missiles is available.

Also, we must not forget that missiles make the individual man more important than ever. Without trained, capable personnel the most modern equipment is useless.

11. Missiles in Space Warfare

Man at last has developed the means to project himself so high and so fast that he can leave the atmosphere entirely and free himself from the grip of the earth's gravity. In the soundless void—if it is a void—of outer space man has the opportunity to explore new worlds, gain new knowledge, and possibly benefit himself in new ways still undreamed of.

But space is a rather hostile environment, and one can reasonably ask why we must probe it.

First, we must explore space because we are curious, because it is there to be explored. Our Maker has given us inquiring minds and has set us in the midst of a fascinating universe which is ours to investigate.

We must also enter space because it offers new opportunities to add to our knowledge of the earth, the solar system, the universe, and perhaps of life itself. This knowledge will benefit men in ways that we already can visualize, and in ways yet to be discovered.

And, finally, we may have to go into space for a tragic reason, surely not the reason for which it was made available to us. A hostile nation may exploit space for its military potential. If space technology (like nearly all other technological developments) is to be used for military purposes by any nation, then we must be prepared to use space to defend ourselves. It is already clear that, should war ever come again between technologically advanced nations, space could play a part in that war. Just how big a part depends upon the time frame, for space technology is growing rapidly.

How could space be used in time of war? The earliest uses could be instrumented orbiting satellites performing several useful functions such as communications, reconnaissance, navigation, and meteorology. Manned military space systems will follow. Man has already joined his instrument carriers and orbited himself. In time manned orbiting stations will be established as well as maneuverable space vehicles, and attack of earth targets from space may be feasible. As these space systems grow in importance, so will the surveillance of space, and defenses will have to be devised. Anti-satellite missiles fired from earth may become effective. To avoid them in time of war, military space systems will have to operate higher and higher above the earth. Finally, the defensive systems may even have to be space based, rather than earth based, in order to reach their targets.

As space systems become more sophisticated and self sufficient, they will still be dependent upon earth support; but the frequency of resupply will diminish, distance from earth will increase, and some systems may even be based on the moon rather than on earth. Unless this newly explored medium can be limited by agreement to peaceful purposes, in time of conflict it will develop into a new theater of war. Thus, instrumented satellites, manned space vehicles, space surveillance, and defense against space vehicles could all have enormous influence in time of war. Let us take a closer look at these.

Military Satellites

Instrumented satellites will be the first systems with wartime application. Fortunately, most of them have peaceful applications as well.

Communication satellites. One of the most fascinating and practical uses of satellites is as orbiting communication relay stations. The communication satellite has an equally promising peacetime value, but its military value lies in its ability to speed up message transmission. For world-wide communication we now use long land lines, submarine cables, and radio. The land and submarine cables can carry only a limited amount of communication traffic, are

Destination: earth orbit. The huge Atlas space booster is shown mated with an Agena satellite vehicle which was designated Samos I after the Atlas hurled it into a polar orbit. (Official U. S. Air Force photograph.)

vulnerable to sabotage, and do not go everywhere they may be needed. Long-distance radio commuciations are extremely susceptible to interference by natural or man-made disturbances. The use of a satellite as a communication relay station promises dramatic improvement in world-wide military communications.

Communication satellites will appear in two basic forms. One is an instantaneous relay or "real-time" satellite. The message sender and receiver both have direct line-of-sight contact with the orbiting vehicle, but they may be thousands of miles apart and otherwise unable to reach each other. The message sender transmits his message to the satellite, and the satellite instantaneously retransmits it to the intended receiver. The higher the satellite above the earth, the more of the earth it can "see" and the greater the range of the communication system. If the communication satellite is put into an equatorial orbit about 22,000 miles high, its period of revolution about the earth will be exactly the same as the period of rotation of the earth itself—24 hours—and the satellite over the equator will appear to be stationary to an observer on the earth. If three such relay satellites are placed in this 24-hour orbit, equally spaced 120° from one another, complete and immediate world-wide communication is possible from almost any two points on earth. The exception is communication with north or south polar regions; for these, equatorial satellites may be tied in with polar satellites and the world-wide communication system thereby completed. The United States' 24-hour-orbit communication-satellite program is known as Project Advent, a Department of Defense project "subcontracted" to the Air Force.

But this system has traffic limitations too: anyone can monitor the transmissions, and not all messages need to be relayed instantaneously. In fact, experience shows that the great volume of military message traffic consists of administrative, lower-precedence messages that can be delayed a few hours in transmission. This type of important but low-precedence traffic is saturating all existing communications means.

The "low"-altitude (100 to 2000 miles) satellite is the answer to this problem. If a memory device (a simple tape recorder to store

A courier in space. The Army's Courier satellite can receive a third of a million words in five minutes, "remember" them, carry them to the other side of the world in less than an hour, and transmit them to the intended receiver without giving an enemy any opportunity to interfere with or read the messages. (U. S. Army photograph.)

messages) is placed in a satellite, the orbiting vehicle can be made to act as a message carrier. The traffic-handling capacity of such a system is enormous. Hundreds of thousands of elements of information can be transmitted to the satellite in a few seconds as it passes over. On the other side of the world, it can be made to spill all the information to its intended receiver. The system can be made highly selective as to whom it serves and when.

The satellites just described are known as active repeaters because they repeat the signals sent to them by retransmitting with a radio carried aboard the satellite. The "Courier" satellite, launched in October 1960, is the current example. The Courier can receive or transmit the entire text of the Bible in ten minutes as it passes over.

A satellite that merely reflects radio waves from earth stations, known as a passive repeater, has promise too. The passive receiver would have to be quite large to give effective reflection, and much more powerful earth transmitters would have to be used. However, passive-satellite relays do not have to carry receiving and transmitting equipment or a power source. Thus a much lighter, longer-lived, and more reliable relay can be placed in orbit. Such a scheme is being investigated by the National Aeronautics and Space Administration. One of the first experiments, called Project Echo, was the launching on August 12, 1960 of a satellite payload which, once in orbit, expanded into a 100-foot-diameter aluminum-coated sphere. Easily spotted with the naked eye, the Echo satellite became a common sight in the night skies.

Intelligence satellites. Another military application of satellites is the intelligence satellite. This type satellite may perform reconnaissance of the earth below or of earth-orbital space, or may provide early warning of an intercontinental missile attack. Reconnaissance of the earth may be accomplished by photography, radar, infrared, electronic interception, and perhaps by other means as well. Photographic reconnaissance, of course, is the most promising but even it presents problems. Clouds or darkness may obscure the subject of interest, as might the enemy himself. The amount of detail the satellite could see 100 or more miles above the observed area is limited too. A 100-mile altitude is probably the lowest that could be used for an orbiting system. At this altitude a camera with a 60-inch focal length will produce a roughly 1:100,000 photograph, or 1 inch on the photo will represent about 1½ miles. This ratio can be improved by using a camera with longer focal length, but this means launching a satellite large enough to carry such a camera as well as a means for getting the picture back to the earth.

In any case, the photograph obtained would have to be processed and returned to earth either by radio or by physical return of the film itself. Radio return may be faster, but return of the film is preferable for high accuracy and resolution of detail. If a large number of photographs are required, physical return of the photographs may prove to be faster then radio transmission, because video scanning of a photograph of high resolution can be very slow.

In spite of the difficulties, photographic reconnaissance satellites will have military uses because any part of the globe can be observed, large areas can be covered rapidly and repeatedly, and proper design and recovery techniques will permit users of the information collected to get their data promptly.

Television techniques in lieu of photographs may have application as well, but the classic focal-length versus altitude problem remains, and the degradation of detail typical of television will also limit its use.

Radar, infrared, and electronic interception may find more application in observing space itself than in observing the earth. If, by any of these techniques, intercontinental missiles could be detected on their launching pads or immediately upon rising into space, precious minutes of early warning would be gained and the system would be worth the cost.

Mapping and meteorological satellites. Other natural extensions of intelligence or information-gathering satellites are mapping and meteorological satellites. Good, accurate maps and precise location of the major land masses of the world with respect to one another are essential in modern war. What value in having an intercontinental missile with a probable error of a few feet, when the target-location error may be many miles?

We can use satellites for mapping in either of two ways. The first is to photograph known and unknown points on the same photograph, thus tying them together. This procedure requires a relatively sophisticated space-borne vehicle, as the photograph must be very accurate, and for best results the film itself should be retrieved. The second method is to track a satellite from two widely separated points, getting simultaneous readings on the location of the satellite with respect to the points. Then by computation the relative location of the two points can be determined. The primary limitation of this system is that ground observers are denied access to certain areas, either for political reasons or because of the extreme difficulty of getting proper equipment there.

The most promising use of the meteorological satellite for the near future is that of obtaining world-wide information on cloud cover. If by photographic means we can observe cloud formations and how they are changing, our ability to forecast weather will be greatly improved. In this case, high resolution is not a requirement since precise boundaries of cloud cover are not important. The United States' "Tiros I" weather satellite, launched by NASA in April 1960, has proved the feasibility of this scheme. It has radioed pictures of cloud cover back to earth by video tape on many occasions.

Navigation satellites. Another valuable application of satellites appears to be in the field of navigation. If a navigator at sea knows the precise location of a satellite at any instant, and can locate his ship precisely with respect to the satellite, a highly accurate all-weather navigation system is possible.

One technique for this form of navigation is causing the satellite to emit continuously a signal of fixed frequency. As it passes over a ship, the frequency will appear to change from a higher frequency than the actual one to a lower. By use of doppler radio technique, the instant the satellite is closest to the ship and the distance between the satellite and the ship at that instant can be determined. The navigator can then use ephemeris tables to locate accurately where the satellite was at the instant it passed closest. Using shipboard computers, he can then locate himself in a very short time. This system can be made to work on a passive satellite as well by creating the signal on shipboard, reflecting it from the satellite back to the ship, and then observing the doppler shift of frequency.

The critical element of this system is accurate ephemerides (predictions of future location in orbit) of the satellite. There is sufficient reason to believe that these can be obtained, but improved space surveillance will have to come first in order to track the navigation satellite accurately. Knowing in detail the path it follows, and studying the forces that influence its orbital motion, scientists will be able to develop highly accurate ephemeris tables. Ship location within a few hundred feet may be possible. Navigation satellites will be useful not only to all naval and commercial vessels having proper equipment aboard, but perhaps even to aircraft as well. Accuracy and all-weather operation far better than any current system is the promise of this project.

Manned Space Systems

As the missions to be performed in space become more complex, and judgment and decision-making processes beyond the capability of machines are required, men will be sent into space to perform them. The orbital flights of Glenn, Titov, and Gagarin proved that man can be sent into space; subsequent developments will necessitate his going into space. A reconnaissance satellite, for example, if manned, could be more effective because the human observer could be more selective in his reporting. He could concentrate his technical aids on areas of primary interest, use power-consuming equipment only when necessary, and so on. If his vehicle were maneuverable, he could change orbits when desired to take a closer look or to see an area not permitted in his original orbit.

Of course, these advantages will have to be weighed against the inherent disadvantages of a system designed to carry and protect human beings. A manned spacecraft must be larger, heavier, and far more complex than an unmanned craft in order to insure passenger comfort, survival in space, and safe return to earth. Even the tiny Mercury capsule, probably the smallest manned satellite that will ever be built, has a base diameter of about 6 feet, is 9 feet long, and weighs about a ton and a half. Much smaller satellites, carrying only instruments, will suffice for some missions. On the other hand, only human beings will be able to perform certain other space missions.

Manned military space systems will be of two basic types. One will be an earth-orbiting space station on which any number of earth-supporting functions could be performed. It will not normally be maneuvered but will adhere to the same orbit. The station might be used to provide reconnaissance, meteorology, navigation, communication relay, and other such services to earth-bound military forces. As a supply base it might store fuel and other supplies for other space vehicles.

The other type of manned space system will be a maneuverable vehicle. It could appear in many forms and have many functions. It could engage in reconnaissance or earth bombardment, attack hostile space vehicles, and rendezvous with, inspect, and repair unmanned satellites.

The first and highly dramatic U. S. project to put a manned orbiting vehicle into space was the NASA Project Mercury flight on February 20, 1962. The primary objective of this pioneer project was manned orbital flight with a safe return. From this flight, NASA began to learn how man would react in a space environment, what his capabilities would be, and how a spacecraft must be designed to allow man not only to survive but to function usefully.

Colonel Glenn's dramatic three-orbit flight is, of course, only the initial U. S. step in manned exploration of space. This one-man capsule can lead to development of more advanced spacecraft much more rapidly than is commonly realized. If we are willing to make the effort and spend the money, we could develop, in five years, highly sophisticated spacecraft capable of maneuver in space and of glide-landing at will on preselected landing fields. The craft could sustain a crew of three of four for days, or even weeks, in space. By 1970 manned spacecraft could go to the moon and return, perhaps even sustain a small permanent lunar outpost.

Before we explore these possibilities, let us first review the remarkable achievement that the Project Mercury flight was.

The Mercury spacecraft (described in Chapter 7) is a cone-shaped capsule that rides atop either a Redstone missile for "short" ballistic boosts or an Atlas for an orbital boost. The first orbital flight, with Colonel Glenn aboard, was conducted almost exactly as planned. The Atlas missile placed the 1-ton manned capsule into orbit from Cape Canaveral, Florida, on an azimuth slightly north of east. The period for one pass around the earth was approximately 89 minutes, and three orbits were made. Reentry of the capsule into the atmosphere was accomplished by firing forward-pointing retro-rockets at the appropriate time, and the final descent of the capsule into the Atlantic Ocean was slowed by parachutes.

This first orbital flight varied in altitude from about 100 to 160 miles. As shown in Fig. 34, orbit was achieved at point *A* about

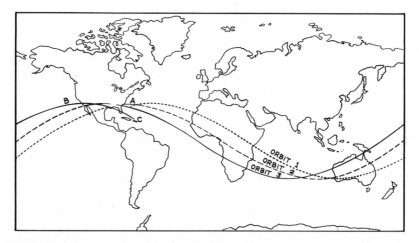

Fig. 34. Map of Colonel John Glenn's triple-orbit flight. Point *A* represents the spot where orbit was achieved; *B* marks the firing of the retro-rockets for descent; and *C* indicates the recovery area upon conclusion of the flight.

500 miles out from the launching pad; the dotted line is the trace of that first orbit. Once in orbit, the manned capsule turned around so that Glenn faced rearward the rest of the trip. At first,

an automatic infrared horizon-scanning system maintained the reverse position and kept the spacecraft in a constant attitude, so that the periscope side always faced the earth, but later the pilot took over manual control using small jets to get the motion desired. The second orbit is represented by the dashed line and the third by the solid line. The third circuit passed just north of Hawaii. A ground station there triggered the firing of retro-rockets when the capsule was at point B. This subtracted about 350 miles per hour from the satellite's velocity of 17,400 miles per hour and it began to lose altitude. As the spacecraft reentered the atmosphere at still more than 17,000 miles per hour, the friction caused the ablative heat shield on its base to glow with the brilliance of a shooting star. Inside, John Glenn was pressed against his couchlike seat with a force equal to eight times his own weight until his capsule slowed to about 600 miles per hour. About 15 minutes and 3000 miles after the retro-rockets fired, the spacecraft deployed a small drogue parachute. At about 10,000 feet, the main parachute opened and the returned satellite was lowered gently into the Atlantic. There, at point C, it was picked up by a destroyer, one of several ships that were standing by to cover the large impact area. The complete sequence of events is shown schematically in Fig. 35.

Emergency procedures had been designed for use in the event a normal three-orbit operation was not accomplished. First of all, the sealed capsule was designed to sustain life for 28 mission hours, plus 12 hours' operation on water or land. A one-week supply of food and water was available. If the capsule had lost pressure, the astronaut's pressure suit would have sustained him long enough to permit him to go on to an established retro-firing point before coming down.

From the outside, America's first spacecraft looks a little like a huge artillery shell and, in a sense, it is one if one thinks of the Atlas or the Redstone as the "artillery." However, one glance inside (see Fig. 33, Chapter 7) dispels the notion at once, for the Mercury capsule is a marvel of instrumentation and devices to control the vehicle and support the astronaut. The pressurized capsule contains an individually form-fitted couch that permits him to tolerate

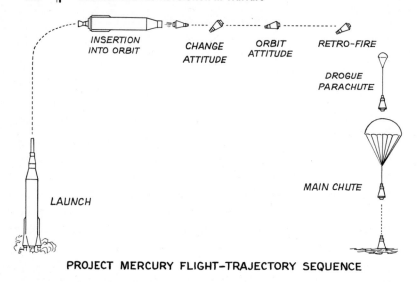

INSERTION
INTO ORBIT

CHANGE
ATTITUDE

ORBIT
ATTITUDE

RETRO-FIRE

DROGUE
PARACHUTE

MAIN CHUTE

LAUNCH

PROJECT MERCURY FLIGHT–TRAJECTORY SEQUENCE

Fig. 35. Schematic of Colonel John Glenn's triple-orbit flight.

the severe acceleration and deceleration. The capsule has a controlled atmosphere, communications, automatic and manual attitude control, and a periscope for observing the ground. There are 7 miles of electrical wiring to connect lights, communications, retro-rockets, power supplies, environmental equipment, and so on.

Colonel Glenn had considerable control over his craft. He was able to talk to many stations down on the planet he was orbiting and had a breathtaking view of the globe through his periscope or his window. He was able to control his attitude manually and did so when the automatic system malfunctioned. He could have fired the retro-rockets at any time and returned to earth.

Every possible contingency had been planned for, and will be in future Mercury orbits. In case of malfunction during the early phase of the launching, emergency procedures permit a land or water landing off Cape Canaveral. Controlled firing of the retro-rockets is intended to assure that other emergency landings during the launching phase will take place in the vicinity of Bermuda or off the northwest African coast. After completion of the first pass, an emergency landing could be made off Charleston, South Carolina, or near Bermuda. An elaborate series of electronic, visual, and acoustical aids used to locate the capsule when it comes down.

If in future Mercury flights there are any emergencies that do not allow firing the retro-rockets at the designated points, in the proper orbit and at the proper altitude, the capsule could land thousands of miles from any planned areas. The possibility is remote, but even this contingency has been taken into consideration. Early descent could place the astronaut in the southern United States or northern Mexico. Late descent could mean Africa or the Indian Ocean. A decision not to wait until an emergency recovery area is within range, but to come down immediately because of fire aboard, physical or psychological reasons, or other emergency could result in a landing almost anywhere between the 33° north and south parallels. Whatever the contingency, there are plans for rescue. If there had been any mishap in Glenn's flight, resulting in his coming down at an unexpected place, rescue teams were poised around the world to go after him. A team of medical specialists were standing by a jet transport aircraft ready to take them anywhere if the call came. Even 30 pints of blood, matched to the astronaut's, were on hand at each rescue station for transfusions if necessary.

Mercury is only the predecessor of the next manned spacecraft. Project Apollo, discussed in more detail in Chapter 12, will lead to manned landings on the moon and on the planets, and to a permanent orbiting manned space station. While NASA programs such as Mercury and Apollo are strictly non-military projects to support man's exploration of the universe, the implications of their military counterparts in the hands of an enemy cannot be ignored.

Another development program that will contribute dramatically to manned space flight is Project Dyna-Soar. The objective of this joint NASA-Air Force project is to obtain hypersonic aerodynamic data on "suborbital" flight. On this project special emphasis will be given to military problems. The Dyna-Soar will be launched into space by a modified Titan booster to a velocity slightly less than that required for orbit. Once separated from its booster, the craft will become a hypersonic glider that will be able to soar through space using both centrifugal force and, when low enough, aerodynamic lift. Such a maneuver is called dynamic soaring, hence the name of the project. The Dyna-Soar will be able to operate from the outer fringes of the atmosphere down to the lower atmosphere, where it can maneuver and glide to a normal aircraft-type landing.

As the project develops, the Dyna-Soar will be given an orbital capability simply by giving it a little more boost. The pilot will have to develop new skills in flying this hypersonic and even orbital craft. In orbit he will be traveling, like the Mercury astronaut, at least 17,400 miles per hour. By the addition and skillful application of power he will be able to change orbit, re-enter the atmosphere when he chooses, and land where he chooses.

Russian manned-flight technology is also well advanced. The Soviets have developed a 5-ton recoverable satellite capable of sustaining human life and have tested it at least four times. Published reports indicate that the first, launched in May 1960 with a human dummy aboard, failed to retro-fire and remained in orbit. The following August the Soviets orbited two dogs, but they perished when the frictional heat of reentry consumed the craft. The fourth try, in February 1961 with dogs and "other biological objects," was apparently quite successful. Russian orbiting of a human passenger first occurred on April 12, 1961, when Major Yuri A. Gagarin successfully orbited the earth in the spaceship "*Vostok.*"

These scientific experiments lead logically to the military question, "Are we about to be presented with a new threat of attack, this time from space?" The answer must be a qualified yes, for the satellite bomber becomes a possibility.

The Satellite Bomber

The first manned orbiting capsule, the *Vostok*, is to future spacecraft what the Wright airplane is to a B–52. Eventually there will

Manned space flight of the near future. An artist's rendering of the launching of an
Air Force Dyna-Soar. A specially adapted Titan ICBM boosts the Dyna-Soar glider toward space.
The booster drops away, leaving the glider in piloted near-orbital flight;
later it glides to a conventional landing. (Official U. S. Air Force photograph.)

be developed a maneuverable space vehicle capable of changing orbit, of rendezvous with other space vehicles, and of returning safely to earth at will. From a military point of view this poses a new threat, for the hostile Communist nations may use such vehicles, if technically feasible, as satellite bombers. Such a weapon system would give a number of advantages to the attacker. The most obvious is ability to attack from a vantage point difficult to reach by our defense. There are no means today to prevent a satellite from doing whatever it wants to do, and the chances are that for the foreseeable future the space offense will stay ahead of the defense by exploitation of ever-increasing altitude, speed, maneuverability, and electronic countermeasures.

A satellite-bomber force could launch its space vehicles deliberately and leisurely in time of peace. It could take full advantage of the most efficient propulsion and guidance systems, ideal weather, and optimum launching sites without concern for enemy countermeasures. The crew, if one were required, could be replaced at regular intervals without returning the satellite bomber to earth by use of a small earth-to-space-and-return "taxi." In bombing, full advantage could be taken of radar, infrared, or line-of-sight methods of guidance; even moving targets, if distinguishable, could be attacked. Thus the threat could change from missiles 5000 miles away to missiles 100 to 200 miles over our heads. The Soviets need only to combine properly techniques learned in their man-in-space program and their Venus program to present this threat. What if the satellite-based Venus rocket were destined not for Venus but for the earth?

To properly evaluate this threat, we must balance against these military advantages the difficulties of satellite "bombardment." First the bomb cannot be "dropped" from orbit. It would simply continue alongside the carrier when released. The warhead must be attached to a space-to-earth missile (STEM) and fired in the direction opposite to orbital motion. Once fired to the rear at even a relatively low speed, the missile would have less than orbital velocity and would begin to spiral in toward the earth. The range from point of firing to target would depend upon the resultant velocity (orbital velocity minus missile velocity) and could vary from zero (vertical drop) to several revolutions around the earth. A zero range would impose an enormous power requirement and would be of no particular value. A 5000-mile range could be created by a rearward velocity of about 1000 feet per second from a low orbit. In these examples, we assume, of course, that the orbit is approximately over the target or can be changed so as to pass over the target. Note also that, although a command to attack an unplanned target immediately could be executed, the time consumed in getting into the proper orbit and in descent of the missile could add up to a considerable delay. A planned surprise attack, however, would give the defender only minutes of warning.

Considering the cost and inherent disadvantages of such a system, from a strictly technical viewpoint the question is, "Can it improve on ballistic missiles?" The guidance requirement would be severe although perhaps not insoluble. It is difficult to assess the relative accuracy of the satellite bomber and the ballistic missile except against a moving target such as a large ship. This exceptional case favors the bomber, because line-of-sight techniques could be used whereas they cannot with ballistic missiles.

The answer also depends in large part upon the relative invulnerability of offensive missile systems. If ballistic missiles eventually could be countered more easily than STEM's, the latter would reign. It is possible that the effectiveness of ballistic missiles will decrease with time; the fixed-launching-site missile will be the first to fade. But mobile, land-based missiles will be more difficult to counter and SLIM's (submarine-launched intracontinental missiles) the most difficult of all. Nevertheless, if the effectiveness of these systems can be sufficiently diminished, and it could happen, STEM's may become a threat to this nation. Then we must find a defense against the space threat.

Space Defense

What do we mean by the term *space defense?* Space defense is the protection of targets on earth from hostile action by satellites or other space vehicles. As for the form it will take, the first space defense will probably feature the use of earth-based missiles similar to the anti-ICBM Nike-Zeus, which has growth potential in this respect. Eventually, space defense will be accomplished in part, or even entirely, by orbiting defensive weapon systems. Novel and radical methods of neutralizing hostile space vehicles will come, and even manned defensive systems may be employed.

The U. S. Air Force research and development Project Saint is pointing toward an orbiting defense system. More accurately, it will be an inspection system, for the concept calls for rendezvous with and inspection of unknown satellites.

Space-defense missiles may sound like the sheerest fantasy, but they may prove to be very effective against lower-altitude vehicles. Consider the target for a moment. It is probably orbital and therefore following a course that can be accurately predicted. It can deviate from orbital flight only for short periods of time; for maneuver requires application of power, and power will be very scarce in space.

These limitations simplify the anti-satellite guidance problem, but can we "see" these targets in space? The answer is, probably so. If the target is sufficiently sophisticated to be a threat, it will probably be large enough to be tracked by powerful radar detection systems, at least in lower orbits. As for method of destruction, the velocity of the target will be so great that even the simple solution of placing material in its path will destroy it. Small particles would act like bullets, for the satellite target would hit them at velocities of thousands of miles per hour.

There will be a "ceiling" above which a space-based system will be more practical than an earth-based. The same techniques that were used to put the target there can be used to put its destroyer there, but some undreamed-of techniques may be used to rendezvous with and attack the offender. So it would seem, as it did in air defense, that one effect of space defense is to drive the target farther and farther away from earth.

When space defense does become necessary, we shall be presented with an extremely complex problem of operational control.

Defense against aircraft and strategic ballistic missiles will still be required, but with additional targets in space how should the total defensive effort be coordinated? The family of weapons that will have to be used to cope with all three types of targets, and the extent to which air, missile, and space defense can be combined, are subjects that deserve serious study.

The problem of defense against air attack versus defense against missiles is already so different that separate weapon systems are mandatory. Target speeds, radar ranges and deployments, warning time, and attack strategies differ markedly for ICBM's and airborne targets. Defense against low-orbit satellites and other low-altitude space vehicles will present problems similar to ICBM defense but will be even more remote from those of airborne attack. Defense against targets deeper in space will bear no resemblance to missile or air defense. Some combination of systems may be possible, but it appears that at least three and probably four distinct weapon systems will be required for the triple threat.

The geographical scope of a space-defense system is another problem. Should space defense ever become necessary, it would probably be accomplished initially over separate continental areas; a single world-wide system might prove too difficult. Successful fire direction (designation of targets to batteries) within areas from a single "world central" will require much greater sophistication of communications, battle management, and control equipment than is foreseeable for several years. However, technological developments in time may permit, or even make mandatory, a world-wide system for space defense. Air and missile defense will more likely remain continental in scope.

Some combination of air, missile, and space defense may be feasible for the near future. Evidence of this feasibility is seen in the assignment of operational control of space surveillance to the North American Air Defense Command (NORAD). Both the Navy's space-surveillance system (SPASUR) and the Air Force space-tracking system (SPACETRACK) report directly to NORAD headquarters for operational control. This system will furnish the commander-in-chief of NORAD with detection, identification, and tracking data of all man-made objects in earth-orbital space that are of potential or actual military concern. Scientific orbital and trajectory information on space vehicles will be handled by the National Aeronautics and Space Administration at its Goddard Space Flight Center, Greenbelt, Maryland.

As space systems advance, however, assignment of the space-defense mission to an existing command may prove awkward. As the space-surveillance system improves its range and target-handling capability, it will prove to the eyes, ears, and voice of the commander who is directing friendly space vehicles. All military space activities will tend to draw farther and farther away from existing commands until a new space command may well be necessary.

Military Space Operations

Should a major war occur within the next few years, and should the Communists choose to exploit space for military purposes, military space systems will have but limited influence. Military space operations would be confined to occasional employment of "first-generation" instrumented satellites supporting military actions on earth. However, by the middle of the decade a number of different types of satellites will be sufficiently developed to provide extremely valuable services to their users and to present a serious threat to their enemy. By 1970, manned and unmanned earth-orbiting weapon systems may be operational, manned explorations may have reached the moon, and bases of operation may even be established on the moon. After 1970, military space operations in time of war would be characterized by actions to gain military supremacy in space, and manned space vehicles could be engaged in combat with one another. Satellite stations and moon bases would have great military significance and would have to be defended. Thus will space have developed into a new theater of war, unless such activity there could somehow be outlawed altogether.

12. Swords to Plowshares

"June 8th mail—3000 letters; destination—Jacksonville, Florida; carrier—missile; prepare for arrival." A routine message far in the future? Not at all; on June 8, 1959 a U. S. Navy Regulus missile was launched from the submarine USS *Barbero* and flew with its mail cargo to a perfect landing at the Naval Auxiliary Air Station near Jacksonville. The joint Navy–Post Office Department experiment may be considered a stunt by some, but since that time the French Government has awarded a contract to investigate the possibility of postal missiles. The Ministry of Postal and Communication Affairs announced that the carrier must hold 660 pounds of mail but did not reveal when or where the system might be used.

This interesting example of peacetime application of missile technology is not an isolated case. As a by-product of guided-missile research and development, great strides have been made in electronics, propulsion, aerodynamics, and many related fields of science and engineering. Yet these advances have only revealed the vast unexplored horizons that still exist.

From a military standpoint, the importance of guided missiles can only grow; yet even in combat form, they can increase the probability of peace. Guided missiles in the hands of a people that hate war can be missiles of peace. In adequate strength and in conjunction with other weapons and courageous men trained to use them, they deter any aggressive nation from initiating a war. Moreover, these swords can be beaten into plowshares.

Missiles in Peacetime

The nonmilitary uses of robot craft are potentially as extensive as the combat uses for which they were originally designed. If, for example, consideration is being given to the wartime use of a reconnaissance missile or a transport missile, cannot one envision similar craft having peacetime applications?

Not that an air-defense missile can be converted overnight into an automatic wild-goose retriever or mail carrier; it cannot. It is principally the individual components of these weapons that have peacetime possibilities. A good part of the money spent on missile development goes into basic studies of propulsion, supersonic aerodynamics, and electronics, and into the development of practical hardware in these fields. Although it is difficult to predict the contributions of these efforts, the possibilities are evident.

Many of the propulsion systems found on missiles may have commercial applications. Ram-jet propulsion, originally developed for missiles, eventually will find application in supersonic commercial transportation.

Knowledge gained in the study of supersonic missile aerodynamics is as important to the piloted-aircraft industry as it is to the guided-missile industry. Supersonic long-distance commercial flights will someday be a normal mode of transportation.

Similarly, many missile guidance and control devices will have nonmilitary applications. If a guidance system can steer a missile accurately to a ground target, could not a similar system be employed to place high-speed commercial aircraft precisely on the runway in any weather? And if a guidance system can continuously predict the future position of a bomber and can guide a missile to insure interception, could not a modification of that same device be used to insure that two planes in danger of collision would not intercept each other? Some commercial aircraft already use collision-warning radar.

The automatic pilots and remote-control devices now being used in missiles will be found increasingly in other types of craft. When it is desirable to make any kind of flight without personnel aboard (for whatever reason), or to control the flight of aircraft at times when human ability is not adequate because of high accelerations, temperatures, or atmospheric conditions, these devices can be put to work. It may be that very high-altitude, rocket-powered weather

Mission: weather report. This Tiros 2 experimental weather satellite
is being readied for flight. Such satellites will photograph cloud cover,
measure heat balance, and contribute to ever-better weather prediction—
perhaps someday even to weather control. (NASA photograph.)

missiles will be used extensively, not only to collect current weather data, but to aid long-range weather prediction as well. Flights over polar regions or into violent storms for weather data could be made by pilotless craft. Missiles already have been used as space boosters for weather satellites.

Some enthusiasts predict regular mail and air-express runs the world over by unmanned supersonic vehicles. By removing the human pilot from the "mail jet," the designer could automatically eliminate a great deal of weight and space-consuming equipment, there solely for the well-being and safety of the pilot. Higher accelerations, velocities, and altitudes would be permissible if the pilot were left at home.

No industry has had its products improved by guided-missile development more than the electronics industry. The reliability, weight and space requirements, and the capabilities of electronic devices have greatly improved because of missile requirements. New and vastly improved automatic computers now exist. The development of a replacement for the vacuum tube, the transistor, was accelerated by demands for high reliability, long life, low power requirements, and small size. As a result, radio and television equipment (less the picture tube) can be shrunk to one-tenth the space of conventional sets and can operate reliably almost indefinitely with a fiftieth of the power now necessary. Because of the need for sending technical information to the ground from a test missile, telemetering developed. Now engineers can observe a piloted aircraft undergoing test maneuvers, know at any instant condition at various parts of the plane, and advise the test pilot accordingly by radio. Telemetering, which one might say is the art of measuring conditions on a vehicle in flight and radioing the information back to earth, has expanded until it is a science in itself.

Missiles have been in use since the end of World War II for upper-atmospheric research. Some means is needed to transport research devices thousands of miles above the earth, and the large guided rocket is the only vehicle capable of accomplishing this task. Goals of millions of miles into space have already been achieved. The objectives of such research are many. Atmospheric density, temperature, and composition, and wind velocities at various levels are sought not only to learn more about the atmosphere itself but also to learn to use it more effectively in flight. Improved study of cosmic rays, the sun, moon, and planets, including the earth itself, is possible with high-altitude research. Today one reads of private industry's plans to orbit commercial communication satellites with government-supplied missiles. Ultimately, the knowledge gained from such experiments will permit travel to other bodies in space.

A multitude of new products and new jobs are emerging from missile research. Ceramic materials developed to protect missiles from the extreme heat of atmospheric friction make excellent heat-resistant containers for kitchen and industry. Powerful miniature batteries for missiles have endless applications in everyday life. Remote-control devices can be used to operate doors, TV sets, air-conditioning systems, and delicate or dangerous machinery at a distance.

Space Travel

One of the most fascinating uses of knowledge gained in guided-missile development is in space travel. Interplanetary flight has been the dream of men for thousands of years. Even before Wan Hu attempted his fateful jaunt, men were predicting flight to the moon.

The thrilling feature of this dream of the ages is that travel beyond the atmosphere of the earth has been accomplished in our time and that manned flight to the moon, and perhaps beyond, is possible in our generation. At last we have a practical means of accomplishing what some people consider the most impractical act known to man—that of leaving earth.

The United States missile program has given, and continues to give, space exploration enormous assistance. The rockets developed as missiles of war provided the starting point. It is only by rocket that man can reach outer space, and the first rockets powerful enough to get there were military. Thus the German V–2 and the

Space flight requires extensive training. An astronaut checks his instrument panel prior to a training "flight" on the human centrifuge at the Aviation Medical Acceleration Laboratory at Johnsville, Pennsylvania. (NASA photograph.)

U. S. Jupiter, Thor, and Atlas have played major roles as space boosters. With the passage of time, boosters specifically designed for space exploration will replace the big missiles, but even then many components will be the same as missile components.

Many space-navigation techniques have grown out of missile guidance systems. In the early stages of space exploration, computers and automatic pilots will continue to solve most of the piloting problems. Indeed, even manned spacecraft will always have such mechanical and electronic aids for the pilot. "Flying by the seat of the pants" just will not work in space. The old description of a person being "so stupid he doesn't know which way is up" can be changed in space to "so stupid he thinks he knows which way is up."

To these examples could be added an almost endless list of developments in metallurgy, electronics, chemistry, environmental control, power sources, and so on—accomplished originally for missiles but now useful for nonmilitary space vehicles. A great part of missile technology is useful in solving the problems of space technology. Let us see what some of these problems are.

Perhaps the most immediate problem is that of overcoming the gravitational field of the earth. The coasting velocity a spacecraft near the earth must have, after its fuel has been expended to escape the powerful gravitational pull, is 36,700 feet per second, or about 25,000 miles per hour (popularly called the escape velocity). Unfortunately, the law of gravity cannot be repealed; it must be overpowered.

Just what is the law of gravity? It is simply that all bodies in space attract one another in proportion to the product of their masses and inversely as the square of the distance between them. If, for example, a weight-conscious lady of 200 pounds could double the distance between herself and the center of the earth by moving to an altitude of 4000 miles above sea level, she would weigh only 50 pounds. If she were still dissatisfied, she would have only to move farther away from the earth. But where would she set her scales?

Man has achieved this escape velocity with the guided missile.

He has orbited the earth, hit the moon, and sent several vehicles into orbit around the sun. With one of the sun orbiters, the NASA "Pioneer V," he maintained radio contact for 22,000,000 miles into space.

But lest he feel that he has conquered the universe, consider for a moment how little of the universe he has explored. A boundless void whose dimensions are beyond the comprehension of man, space is a hostile medium about which he still knows very little. What he does know is awesome enough. The nearest heavenly body is the moon, about 239,000 miles away, but the earth and its natural satellite is only a part of the solar system of one sun and nine planets.

The outermost planet, Pluto, is about 4,000,000,000 miles from the sun, an insignificant distance compared to the galaxy to which the solar system belongs. Using the astronomical unit of distance, the light-year (the distance light travels in one year—63,200 times as far as from earth to sun), our galaxy of millions of stars swirling in a great disk shape is at least 100,000 light-years in diameter. But this galaxy is only one of an endless number of galaxies. At least a billion are in the region of space observable from the earth, each galaxy an average of 2,000,000,000 light-years from the next.

Just to go to the nearest star within our own galaxy, Alpha Centauri, defies the ingenuity of man. This star is 4 light-years away, which means that merely to send a radio signal and get an answer would take 8 years transmission time. To go there at rocket velocities attainable today would require 100,000 years. Perhaps with nuclear or ion rockets, the time could be shortened to 1000 years unless the erosion of collisions with astral dust particles destroyed the rocket. Man will do well to explore the solar system in the next 50 to 100 years, but when he has done so he will have visited only an infinitesimal portion of our Maker's universe.

And explore it he probably will, first in earth satellites, then by visits to the moon, and finally by instrumented or even manned visits to other planets. The nature of his first satellite trip was described in Chapter 11.

An artificial satellite must be established well away from the earth for several reasons. It must be above the atmosphere to avoid atmospheric drag and heating. Also, the higher the orbit the more of the earth it can "see," the less shading by the sun, and the less disturbance by the earth's not-quite-spherical shape.

The potential advantages of the satellite station are several, space-travel enthusiasts say. From this platform beyond the atmosphere scientists could obtain information on solar heat, cosmic rays, and meteor bombardment, and could plan the next step, travel to the moon and beyond. The space station itself could be used as the launching base for such travel. Vastly improved observation of the universe and the earth will also be possible from the space station because there will be no interference from the atmosphere that blankets our sphere.

To build a manned space station will be no small feat of engineering. First of all, materials for the installation will have to be hauled into space by "freighter" missiles. Navigation will have to be extremely precise or the freighters, traveling at miles-per-second speeds, will never be able to get their cargoes in the same orbit. The space station will have to be assembled by men in pressurized and oxygen-supplied space suits; they could not survive unprotected. One idea for the design of the man-made satellite is to build it in the shape of a giant doughnut 150 feet or more in diameter. When it is revolved slowly, centrifugal force will substitute for the effect of gravity within it. The ring would be pressurized and air conditioned, and solar heat would be harnessed to generate electric power. These problems have been worked out in considerable detail, but there are many unknowns yet to be determined.

To the Moon and Mars

Manned flight to the moon is within man's grasp. In May 1961 the President of the United States recommended to the Congress that the project be established as a national goal. Congress approved, and the program is now under way. It is only a matter of time until the first expedition lands; the only real unknowns are when the landing will take place and the nationality of the explorers.

Because of the political, scientific, and military stature that will come to the nation that first sends men to the moon and returns them safely, it is important that the United States be first. However, an additional goal should be the establishment of a manned lunar outpost. Given sufficient impetus, a permanently manned outpost could be established within a year or two of the first landing. Planning for the outpost should be done concurrently with development of the transportation. By establishing the first lunar outpost, the United States would have unquestioned and continuing pre-eminence in space.

Politically, the project has significant overtones. Witness the political use made of Gagarin, the first astronaut to orbit the earth. Although its program has probably slipped somewhat, the Soviet Union in a propaganda broadcast once announced that the fiftieth anniversary of the present government (in 1967) will be celebrated by Soviet citizens on the moon. Successful exploitation of space by the Soviets could contribute greatly to Communist world leadership. The establishment of the first lunar outpost would be of enormous political advantage.

Study of the universe, of the moon, and of the space environment will all be aided by scientific effort on the moon. Perhaps the most promising scientific advantage is the usefulness of a moon base for further explorations into space. Materials on the moon itself may prove to be valuable and commercially exploitable. Communications may be greatly improved by the use of a moon-based relay station.

Eventually there may be a military requirement as well for the manned outpost on the moon. The full extent of the military potential cannot be predicted, but it is probable that observation of the earth and of space vehicles from the moon will prove to be highly advantageous. With a moon-to-earth base line, space surveillance by triangulation promises great range and accuracy. Current earth-based surveillance systems are inadequate for deep space operations. The employment of moon-based weapon systems against earth or space targets may prove to be feasible and necessary.

Two broad problem areas must be tackled. One is the design

and construction of the lunar outpost; the other is the transportation. The outpost itself may be developed in stages by using the landing vehicle and its empty fuel tanks as living quarters. It may be necessary to construct the dwelling underground in holes or caves of the moon rather than above the surface. Going underground, besides reducing to a minimum the requirements for construction material from the earth, will result in a lessening of the temperature extremes (200° F below zero to 250° above) that will be experienced on the surface. An additional benefit will be the decrease in vulnerability to meteorites and high-energy bombardment. A structure could be pressurized underground with plastic materials expanded against the sides of caves, or empty rocket-fuel tanks could be buried to provide shelter. From this closed environment further expansion of the outpost could be accomplished.

The transportation project has already been initiated. In 1961 the National Aeronautics and Space Administration undertook what will become the greatest scientific and engineering achievement in the history of the nation. The goal of NASA's Manned Lunar Landing Program is to send, before the end of the decade, three men to the moon and return them safely.

Flight to the moon will be the greatest adventure of the century, but many problems must be solved before this dream of the ages becomes a reality. Perhaps the biggest problem of all is to determine how to give a multiton payload the necessary seven miles per second escape velocity with the power plants that can be built. The payload must be big enough to house and protect the passengers and to carry sufficient propulsion stages and fuel to maneuver in space, execute a landing on the moon, take off again, and land on earth. The spacecraft NASA intends to use for this purpose, called the Apollo, will weigh about 75 tons.

Several alternatives are possible. The trip could be made by direct flight to the moon, requiring an enormous booster rocket, or by intermediate orbital steps. The orbital method involves the rendezvous of two or more components in orbit to assemble a lunar vehicle or to refuel exhausted tanks. Any solution imposes a staggering propulsion requirement: millions of pounds of thrust. To solve this propulsion requirement, NASA is designing and building a family of three different rockets, all huge by today's standards. These are identified as the Saturn, Advanced Saturn, and Nova.

The Saturn, under development since 1958, represents the first truly large booster designed exclusively for space travel. The first stage of the Saturn is a liquid-propellant (oxygen and kerosene) eight-engine rocket with a total thrust of 1,500,000 pounds. The second stage, a liquid-oxygen and liquid-hydrogen combination, will have six engines and a thrust of 90,000 pounds. The entire rocket will stand perhaps 200 feet high, depending upon the length of the payload, and is over 20 feet in diameter at the base. This is the baby of the family!

In addition to the Saturn, NASA has already started development of the second rocket, the Advanced Saturn. This will become the workhorse of the lunar project, because it will be the first rocket able to give the 75-ton Apollo the necessary velocities. Five huge F–1 engines, each having 1,500,000 pounds of thrust, will provide the power for the first stage. The F–1 has already been developed and has achieved this thrust. The first stage alone will be 140 feet long and 33 feet in diameter, and will carry 2000 tons of propellant. The second stage for this giant will be a five-engine liquid-hydrogen–liquid-oxygen rocket with a total thrust of 1,000,000 pounds. This combination is capable of putting 100 tons into a low earth orbit. A third stage is planned also for some missions. This threesome will stand 270 feet tall.

But why stop here? The Nova first stage will use eight engines of 1,500,000 pounds thrust each for a total of 12,000,000 pounds. Forty-five feet in diameter, it will burn 3400 tons of propellant. A 5,000,000 pound thrust second stage is contemplated and a third, identical to the Advanced Saturn third stage, will have a 200,000-pound thrust.

Solid-propellant rockets are being investigated as alternate solutions for some of this series. They offer the advantages of simplicity and ability to fire at the instant desired.

Destination moon, Mars, or Venus. NASA's Saturn, shown in
assembled form, will place 10 tons in low orbit and send significant payloads to near-by planets.
It is almost 200 feet long and will weigh 500 tons at take-off. (NASA photograph.)

Now let us examine how NASA plans to use these rockets. One of the most promising rendezvous alternatives being investigated involves the use of two Advanced Saturns. One will place the three-man Apollo spacecraft into orbit and the other will bring an additional propulsion stage into orbit for the Apollo. This stage will be used to give the Apollo earth-escape velocity and is called the escape stage. The Apollo itself consists of three compartments, or modules as NASA calls them. The nose compartment is called the command module and carries the astronauts and control instruments. A middle section contains life-support equipment and a propulsion unit for taking off from the moon. This unit is also capable of returning the craft to earth at any time, should an emergency develop and it be decided to abandon the mission. A third section at the rear, called the lunar-landing module, will provide the power for putting the Apollo into orbit around the moon and for easing it gently to the lunar surface. Total weight—75 tons! Hence, the need for the 7,500,000-pound thrust of the Advanced Saturn to lift it into orbit.

The escape stage will be launched first and fully checked out by remote control, while in orbit, to assure that it is in perfect condition. About twenty-four hours after the launch of the escape stage, the three astronauts will take off in the Apollo to catch this propulsion unit and fasten it to their spacecraft. The timing of this second launch will be extremely critical, because the object with which they must rendezvous will be orbiting at a velocity of five miles per second. A four-second delay at launch time will put them twenty miles behind the propulsion stage! The plan calls for getting within twenty miles, so that only a small amount of power will have to be expended to maneuver up to the escape stage. Once the two components are together, careful maneuvering and deft workmanship will be necessary to assemble them into a single unit.

When the assembled moon rocket reaches a precise point in the orbit for departure to the moon, the astronauts will fire the escape stage. This stage, burning for about seven minutes, will increase their velocity from five to seven miles per second, and escape velocity will be achieved. Once this stage has fired, it has no further use and will be jettisoned.

After a 2½-day flight to the vicinity of the moon the spacecraft will maneuver into a low orbit and then, in a rocket-motors-forward attitude, ease carefully down to the moon's surface. The rocket motors will have to be used for braking action because there is no atmosphere to help slow the fall. Special legs will be extended to keep the rocket upright when it touches the surface.

Assuming all goes well, the astronauts will remain about twenty-four hours for limited scientific investigations and exploration. They will probably be able to leave the rocket and walk about for short periods in special space suits.

Take-off from the moon will use up most of the remaining rocket fuel. After a 2½-day glide back to earth, very careful maneuvering will cause the Apollo to pass within a few hundred miles of the earth and swing into an orbit around it. Finally a gradual descent, similar to the Mercury trajectory, will be executed and a parachute will lower the three-man command module to earth.

One gulps nervously just to think of all the things that could go wrong. Yet by the time a flight such as this takes place, all aspects of the trip will have been carefully worked out and rehearsed exhaustively under actual or simulated conditions. For example, the rendezvous will have been practiced in space many times before the decision to fire the escape stage and go on to the moon. A few steps, however, will be almost impossible to simulate. For example, the project will depend upon pilot skill, on the first try, in getting the spacecraft into orbit around the moon, in landing on the lunar surface, and in hitting the right orbit upon return to earth. In each case the first time must be right.

This flight will be preceded by preliminary space ventures to gain the necessary knowledge and skills for the moon trip. The first, a three-orbit Mercury flight, has already been accomplished. The Mercury flights next will be extended into day-long orbits to learn more about the effects of prolonged periods of weightlessness. The little 1½-ton Mercury capsule will then turn the program over to its bigger brothers. Next, NASA will learn how to rendezvous equipment in space and assemble it. The "Gemini" space-craft, a three-ton, two-man vehicle, will be used for this phase. The Gemini, able to orbit for a week or more with two passengers aboard, will also be used to study the effects of long-duration weightlessness. It will be hurled into orbit by the Air Force missile, Titan II.

Earth-orbital Apollo flights, boosted by the 1,500,000-pound thrust Saturn, will begin in the 1964–1966 time period. The Advanced Saturn will then send the Apollo on circumlunar flights, and in the 1968–1970 period, by use of the rendezvous technique, the combined payloads of two Advanced Saturns will carry three men to land on the moon.

A direct flight to the moon without the use of an intermediate orbital step is also being planned. For this mission the giant Nova, with its first-stage thrust of 12,000,000 pounds, will have to be used. The Nova will give the Apollo spacecraft escape velocity by firing successive stages; once this velocity is achieved, the re-mainder of the flight is identical to the rendezvous method. Use of the Nova for lunar flights will probably come after the Advanced Saturn but, in the event of unexpected difficulties with the orbital-rendezous approach, the Nova will be used for the first landing.

The Nova will have other uses as well. It will be able to place very large space stations in orbit and carry materials for construct-ing a lunar outpost. It will be large enough to carry a nuclear second stage that will double its payload capacity. Nuclear pro-pulsion pays off when a sufficiently large stage can be lifted.

It is most unfortunate that this greatest adventure in the history of man, exploration of the moon, is handicapped by hostility be-tween nations. If the efforts of the Soviet Union and the United States could be combined, manned flight to the moon could prob-ably be accomplished several years earlier than it will be by either nation doing it alone—and with much less economic strain.

With their existing high-thrust boosters, the Soviets have an enormous propaganda opportunity; space accomplishments are dramatic and bring open admiration from all other nations. By deliberately scheduling its program to beat that of the United States in each space development, Russia can assure itself of a series of propaganda victories. The Soviet Union placed the first man in earth orbit; it will probably make the first manned orbit of the moon. Whether the first man to land safely on the moon will be Russian or American is squarely up to us. With the Saturn-Nova family, we can begin to compete after 1965. And whether we like it or not, a good portion of the world's population may be greatly influenced on the basis of this project alone in deciding which nation has the better form of government and way of life.

Travel to other planets will be much more difficult to accomplish. Both Mars and Venus are good candidates, with Mars the more promising. It has an atmosphere that includes some oxygen and provides a pressure, at "Mars level," about one-half of our sea-level pressure. The force of gravity will be considerably less, so walking around should not be too laborious. The predicted travel time used to present a serious obstacle, but now it looks as though the trip could be made in 100 days or less by the time we get around to attempting it in the 1970's.

Travel to the moon and the planets is a fascinating goal for mankind; however, there is more to space exploration than reaching other bodies. The first stage of exploration is earth-orbital flight. Project Mercury has furnished the first manned vehicle in this stage, the two-man Gemini will provide the second, and the three-man spacecraft project, Apollo, will furnish the third. By these programs NASA will determine the ability of man to contribute usefully to space exploration and learn how to go on to the moon and to the planets.

Earth-orbital instrumented satellites are a part of this stage as well. Improved meteorological and communication satellites and orbiting solar, geophysical, and astronomical observatories all will take part.

The second stage, which will be concurrent with the first, could be identified as exploration of cislunar space. We need to know much more about the environment of space this side of the moon in order to continue with a logical program. A problem of serious concern for manned flight beyond low orbits is that of radiation in space. The radiations of the Van Allen belt, of cosmic rays, and of solar flares must be well understood before man is exposed to them.

The third stage of space exploration is related to the moon and includes lunar-impact projects, lunar orbits, and finally lunar landings. The Soviet space program is already into this stage without awaiting completion of the first two. As previously mentioned, the U. S. Project Apollo includes a lunar-circumnavigation stage.

Stages for exploration of translunar space can hardly be identified; there are too many unknowns. Certainly Mars and Venus will be frequent targets in the 1970's. As for when an earth-man might walk on another planet, one person's guess is as good as another's. There is nothing in sight so far that will preclude its happening some day, surely before the end of the century. Eventually, instrumented vehicles will reach all planets in the solar system. However, beyond that and on to the stars lies an abyss of space that will not be crossed until man has made some radically new discoveries.

Despite all difficulties, man is determined to "conquer" space and stands a fair chance to conquer cislunar space in our own generation. It is the most fantastic and challenging travel adventure man has dreamed of. If achieved, it will be in great part a direct outgrowth of today's guided-missile program.

On War and Peace

To many persons the very term *guided missile* connotes the horror of total push-button warfare and the obliteration of modern civilization. Possibly some even have the notion that the advancement of some branches of science should be halted because of the destructive tools that those branches are capable of producing. Unfortunately, it is almost inevitable that a major technological achievement will have some military potential in time of war. Indeed, many of the most important technological accomplishments have come into being because of war. Moreover, under threat of attack, a nation which followed a deliberate policy of failing to arm itself with the best weapons obtainable would only invite that attack.

Providing the armed forces of a nation with missiles and other modern weapons does not mean that war is inevitable. Where is the mature, intelligent American, in or out of uniform, who wants war? Not one will say that war provides any final solution to world problems. The only lasting steps toward permanent peace are educational, moral and spiritual, and economic. Yet military strength is needed initially to maintain freedom and to permit these peaceful means to function at all. To strip a peace-loving nation of modern weapons in an effort to eliminate war would be as foolish as to disarm a city's police force to eliminate crime.

The military plans of the United States include maintaining in constant readiness skilled and courageous leadership, trained men and women, and the most modern weapons—including missiles of all types—to provide an effective deterrent force to discourage any would-be aggressor from risking war, and to insure the defeat of that nation should war be forced upon us. These military preparations do not include the gathering of huge stockpiles of weapons that would soon become obsolete, nor do they include the holding of great masses of men under arms. The armament program, of which missile development, production, and deployment is an integral part, is designed to give strength without disruption of national economy in order that permanent steps toward peace may be undertaken.

From a technological point of view, it appears that at no time in history has the establishment of world-wide peace been more important than now. The world has entered a period during which total war cannot be really successful. The winner would scarcely be better off than the loser. Therefore an imperialistic nation will be forced to confine military conflict to small local actions or to resort entirely to more subtle means. Accordingly, let us not become so preoccupied with the nuclear weapons that we find ourselves attacked from behind with that subsonic, man-powered bayonet.

A most lucid combination of the lessons of history and the impact of technology has been made by the renowned historian Arnold Toynbee. He shows how improved means of travel and communication forced city-states to amalgamate into nation-states. The penalty for a city's remaining independent was defeat and absorption into a nation-state. Similarly, the nation-states in the modern air age have shrunk, timewise, until the supranational state has become desirable both for normal peacetime existence and for adequate strength in time of war; hence the timely union of the North Atlantic Treaty Organization powers (and, we might add, the founding of the United Nations). Eventually, the brilliant scholar reasons, rapidly advancing means of transportation and communication will enforce a world-state, either peacefully or by war. The final result is inevitable, he concludes; men must choose by which means.

Men must also choose what kind of world—Communist or democratic. The big race is on; not just the race for space, for missile supremacy, or for the highest production rate. Communism and democracy are at war to win men's minds. It is a war that takes many forms, and the Communists are determined to win. They are intelligent and energetic, and are as dedicated to their cause as the most committed devotees of any religion. The strategic goal of Communist Russia is world domination; apparent changes in actions, tools of conflict, or policy are only tactical maneuvers toward this strategic goal. To the ignorant, the oppressed, the underprivileged, and the naive, the Communist philosophy is an appealing ideology because it offers promise of relief. The ideology of freedom under democracy is the superior one, but it will win out only by the most steadfast and courageous efforts. For the United States citizen this means military and economic aid abroad, taxes, and the selling of democracy everywhere.

Complicating this situation is a rapidly expanding population in a world that may be diminishing in natural resources. One reads that world population is increasing at a rate of 1.7 percent per year. In 1950, 2.5 billion people were living on this earth. In the year 2000, the figure will have almost doubled; and by 2050, the world will have 6 to 8 billion inhabitants. Some informed geologists say this 6 to 8 billion may inherit an earth which has already given up most of its easily obtainable coal, oil, and gas.

We are presented with enormous challenges in the race for men's minds, in almost every direction we look. The contest is particularly avid in the field of science and engineering, and in this vital area we are going to be outdistanced unless radical changes occur. The key to future scientific superiority is scientific education today. The Soviet Union well recognizes this. Today there are perhaps 1,200,000 scientists and engineers in the United States and 800,000 in Russia; but this is not a static situation, for it is changing rapidly in favor of the Russians. In 1950, the United States graduated 50,000 engineers while the Soviets graduated 30,000. In 1955, the figures were just reversed, and in 1960, the National Science Foundation estimated that this country graduated 37,000 engineers compared to the Soviet 106,000.

Science is taking on greater significance each year. It is estimated that of all the money spent in scientific effort in the entire history of the country, more than half of it has been spent since 1950.

Through science our neighbors on the other side of the earth are being drawn inexorably closer to us. They live only a few hours away, and every day we are better able to observe one another's ways of life, standards of living, and spiritual values. Soon we will communicate directly with our world neighbors through world-wide television, and they will see the many privileges of democratic life. Who will deny the underprivileged the fruits of research in medicine, chemistry, electronics, and mechanics that we now enjoy?

Since World War II more than half the world's population has received political independence for the first time in centuries. For the most part they are behind the Western World in acquiring what we call the material needs of everyday living. To set about raising their standard of living would bring a sound, long-term world prosperity, the like of which the world has not seen. But perhaps such peaceful prosperity waits on technology, first by the use of modern communication to prove the need to the masses, then by providing the means to accomplish it.

The military implications of modern technology are sobering. These are momentous times in which we live and the Communist threat is very real; we are actually at war now. Faced by a ruthless government that respects only power, we must have an adequate military posture. There are many nonmilitary actions that we must take as well, but to be successful we must take them in an atmosphere of strength. We prefer negotiation to war; yet we will gain no more from the Communists by negotiation than we are capable of gaining by military action.

This nation has an excellent military posture today, but there are areas in which we can improve. Perhaps our most important need is mobility more nearly commensurate with our firepower. Strategic and tactical mobility can and should be greatly enhanced, principally by increased use of aircraft designed for the purpose.

Another pressing need is improved missile defense. The greatest single thing we can do now to deter nuclear war, in addition to what we have already done, is to build missile-defense shelters. The shelters should emphasize radiation protection, but blast and thermal effects can be greatly reduced as well. An active antimissile defense system must be established too.

We must also take care that we do not overlook conventional means of war. The Communist exploitation of nationalism, hunger, and economic stress in underdeveloped countries produces forms of conflict that no missile can counter. This is the great paradox of military technology.

When modern technology can work in a peaceful atmosphere, new heights of progress hitherto undreamed of can be reached. It is both a privilege and a challenge to live in these times of outstanding scientific achievements. Surely the human race ultimately will be better because of these achievements, guided missiles not excepted.

Appendix A

THE 25-YEAR MISSILE REVOLUTION (1935–1960)

Year	Event
1935	German Army began development of test missiles leading to V–2 rocket.
1940	U. S. Army Air Corps established guided-missile program.
1944	German V–1 and V–2 operational.
1945	U. S. Navy Bat (air-to-ship missile) operational.
1947	U. S. Army Corporal fired (first completely guided ballistic missile).
1949	U. S. Army made first penetration into space, 250 miles altitude, with two-stage rocket.
1951	U. S. Army Nike-Ajax destroyed aerial target (first successful surface-to-air missile intercept).
1956	U. S. Air Force Falcon (air-to-air missile) operational.
1957	Great Britain announced policy of replacing all combat aircraft with missiles.
	Russia placed first artificial satellite in orbit.
1958	U. S. Army Nike-Hercules destroyed high-altitude, high-supersonic aerial target (altitude, 100,000 feet; Mach 3 +).
	U. S. Air Force Atlas (intercontinental ballistic missile) fired successfully full range.
1959	Russian missile-launched space probe escaped earth's gravitational field.
	Russian *Lunik II* placed first man-made object on moon.
1960	U. S. Army Nike-Hercules destroyed Corporal (first successful intercept of a ballistic guided missile).

Appendix B

GLOSSARY OF COMMONLY USED GUIDED-MISSILE TERMS

Accelerometer–An instrument that measures acceleration. Generally employed as three units to measure acceleration in three dimensions, it can be used to measure distance traveled.

Aerodynamics–That branch of fluid mechanics dealing with the study of motion of air and other compressible fluids, and of bodies in those fluids.

Aeropause–A region from about 60 to 90 miles above the earth between air and space. In this region particles are sufficiently dense to provide appreciable drag to vehicles, but insufficient lift for aerodynamic support. The medium is neither air nor space.

Afterburner–A device in a turbojet engine behind the turbine that increases thrust by injecting and burning additional fuel in the jet stream.

AICBM–Anti-intercontinental ballistic missile. An SAM designed to counter ICBM's.

Air space–The region from the earth's surface to about 60 miles altitude (the maximum altitude for aerodynamic lift), occupied by air (gas in the normal 80:20 nitrogen–oxygen ratio).

ALBM–Air-launched ballistic missile. An ASM with ballistic-type trajectory.

Attitude, guided missile–The orientation of a missile with respect to some reference such as the earth's surface, to the vertical, or to a target.

Axial-flow turbojet–A gas-turbine engine with compressor composed of multiple blades attached to a central axis. The air flow is parallel to the axis and permits an engine design of small frontal area.

Beam rider–A guided missile having internal equipment that detects and maintains its position in a beam of electromagnetic energy.

Booster–An auxiliary propulsion system attached to a missile to obtain high acceleration at take-off. Usually it is automatically detached after its fuel is consumed.

Canard–A type of aerodynamic design utilizing control surfaces on the forward part of a missile frame ahead of the lifting surfaces.

Chain reaction–A continuous process of fission or fusion. The energy and particles released by fission and/or fusion cause more fissions and/or fusions to take place in the active material.

Chemosphere–The layer of atmosphere from about 20 miles to 60 miles above the earth.

Cislunar–This side of the moon, or within the volume created by rotating the orbit of the moon about an axis in its plane containing the earth.

Combustion–The actual ignition and burning of a fuel-and-oxidizer combination. It may be spontaneous or it may require auxiliary ignition.

Control, guided missile–The means of maintaining or changing the course of a missile.

Crash project–A drastically telescoped development program, the urgency of which does not permit normal sequential steps to be taken.

Diffuser–A channel of varying cross-sectional area used to decrease fluid velocity and increase pressure. For subsonic flow the area increases in the direction of the flow; for supersonic flow, it decreases. It is used in the intakes of air-breathing engines.

Doppler effect–An apparent change in frequency of a signal caused by relative motion of the source and the receiver. It can be used to determine the velocity of a missile by placing a radio-frequency source in the missile and a receiver on the ground, or by reflecting a ground-source signal from a moving missile.

Drag–The total forces on a missile, created by the fluid in which it travels, that oppose the motion of the missile.

Drone–An unmanned aircraft, usually controlled remotely, often used in activities where the presence of human beings is undesirable, such as for antiaircraft targets and dangerous flights. Also called pilotless aircraft.

Elevator–A movable airfoil, normally in the horizontal plane, used to control the pitch of a missile.

Exosphere–The outermost layer of the atmosphere, of undetermined thickness, beginning at about 600 miles above the earth and extending outward until indistinguishable from space. It is characterized by gaseous particles so widely spaced that they move freely without interference from one another.

FBM–Fleet ballistic missile. A ship-launched SSM with ballistic-type trajectory.

Flame holder–A device usually found in air-breathing jet engines to stabilize combustion. The high velocity of the air within an engine would extinguish the flame without such a device.

Guidance–The means of determining the proper flight path of a missile and of moving the missile on that path.

Guided missile–An unmanned vehicle, the trajectory of which is capable of being altered by mechanisms within the vehicle. The mechanisms may be controlled from within or without the vehicle.

ICBM–Intercontinental ballistic missile. An SSM with ballistic-type trajectory and a maximum range of 5000 miles or more.

Ionosphere–The layer of atmosphere lying from about 60 miles above the earth to about 250 miles. It is characterized by widely spaced atoms of oxygen and nitrogen as well as ions and free electrons.

IRBM–Intermediate-range ballistic missile. An SSM with ballistic-type trajectory and a maximum range of about 1500 miles.

Kiloton–One thousand tons. A unit of measure of explosive power usually applied to nuclear weapons, it is equivalent to the explosive power of 1000 tons of conventional high explosive.

Lunar operations–Operations on or in the vicinity of the moon.

Mach number–The ratio of the velocity of a body in a medium to the local velocity of sound in that medium.

Mass ratio–The ratio of total take-off weight of a missile to the weight after all fuel is consumed.

Mesosphere–A layer of the earth's atmosphere extending from about 250 to 600 miles altitude. The region contains mesons and other cosmic particles.

MRBM–Medium-range ballistic missile. An SSM with ballistic-type trajectory and a maximum range of about 950 miles.

Near space–That region of space within one earth radius, or 4000 miles from the earth's surface.

Nozzle–A tube of varying cross section used on jet engines to increase the velocity of the exhaust stream. Normally it narrows to a minimum cross section at a point called the throat, then expands to the exhaust opening.

Nuclear fission–A nuclear transformation in which a heavy nucleus (with a large number of nucleons) is split into two or more nuclei. The nucleons in the resulting nuclei are in a more efficient combination (lower energy), and therefore mass is transformed into released energy.

Nuclear fusion–A nuclear transformation in which two or more light nuclei (with few nucleons) are combined into a single large nucleus. The nucleons in the resulting nucleus are in a more efficient combination (lower energy), and therefore mass is transformed into released energy.

Outer space–That region of space beyond one earth radius, or 4000 miles from the earth's surface.

Pilotless aircraft–An aircraft equipped to fly without the use of a human pilot. In this sense also called a drone.

Pulse jet–A simple air-breathing jet engine that produces thrust by the intermittent intake and combustion of air and fuel.

Ram jet–A simple air-breathing jet engine that obtains compression by the ramming effect of air when the missile is in rapid motion. No mechanical compressor is needed.

Regenerative cooling–A method of cooling a liquid-fuel rocket motor by passing the fuel or oxidizer through a cooling jacket about the motor before the fluid is fed into the combustion chamber.

Satellite–A space vehicle having position and velocity appropriate for it to orbit many times around the center of reference.

Shock wave–A moving boundary between two regions of differing density, pressure, temperature, and velocity; created in a compressible fluid such as air, usually by relative motion in the fluid of a body faster than the speed of sound.

SLIM–Submarine-launched intracontinental missile. A submarine-launched SSM with ballistic-type trajectory, having a maximum range sufficient to reach any target within a continent from adjacent waters (about 1800 miles).

Sonic velocity–That velocity equal to the speed of sound in a medium. In air at sea level, it is approximately 764 miles per hour (1120 feet per second); at 40,000 feet, approximately 664 miles per hour.

Space–That portion of the universe outside of but not including heavenly bodies and their atmospheres. The lower limit of space with respect to the earth is that altitude at which atmospheric drag appreciably affects the orbiting characteristics of earth satellites, about 90 miles.

Space defense–The protection of terrestrial installations and regions from attack by satellites and other space vehicles.

Space offense–Offensive operations against terrestrial targets from space; activity against enemy materiel or personnel on earth, sea, or air from a satellite, other space vehicle, or lunar station.

Space surveillance–The detection, tracking, identification, and cataloguing of all satellites and other space vehicles. Space surveillance does not concern itself with the processing of data from satellites—for example, with electronic intelligence and photographs from a reconnaissance satellite or messages from a communication satellite.

Space vehicle–A man-made object designed to travel in space beyond the earth's atmosphere. The vehicle may be controlled or uncontrolled, manned or unmanned, orbital or nonorbital. The term does not include ballistic missiles that traverse space enroute to earth targets or antiballistic-missile missiles.

Specific impulse–Pounds of thrust developed per pound of propellant consumed per second. A measure of the efficiency of a rocket engine.

SRBM–Short-range ballistic missile. An SSM with ballistic-type trajectory and a maximum range of about 62 miles.

STEM–Space-to-earth missile. A missile launched from a vehicle in space and directed to a target on earth.

Stratosphere–The layer of atmosphere from about 6 miles to about 20 miles above the earth. It is characterized by usually steady, predictable winds and a temperature of about 67° F, except near the outer edge where the temperature rises to about 170° F.

Telemetering–Transmission by radio from detectors of physical phenomena (temperature, pressure, and the like) to read-out equipment remotely located. The measuring instruments themselves usually are aboard satellites or missiles with the actual dials located at a ground station.

Thrust–The reactive force, usually expressed in pounds, exerted by a jet-propulsion system. For a vertically launched missile the thrust must exceed the entire weight of the missile.

Translunar–Beyond the moon.

Troposphere–The lowest layer of atmosphere extending from sea level to about 6 miles. It is characterized by rapidly decreasing pressure and temperature with increasing altitude.

Turbojet–An air-breathing jet engine that obtains compression by a mechanical compressor.

Index